THE LEFT OF
A COUNTRY & WHAT'S LEFT

THE LEFT OF A COUNTRY & WHAT'S LEFT

AMERICA'S DECLINE

Lori Buelow

Indy Pub

DEDICATION

This book is dedicated to those who cherish "Truth" and decide to follow their conscience in the presence of God and do what they know to be right.

DISCLAIMER

Even though the author and publisher have made every effort to ensure the content in this book is current at the time of printing, and even though this publication is meant to give accurate information about the topic it covers, no liability is accepted by the author or publisher for any potential loss, impairment caused by oversight or mistakes whether due to default, mishap, or any other cause.

Contents

Contents

Contents

Introduction

AMERICA IN DECLINE

Introduction

There are many ways that a country can lose its freedoms, but the most common is when the government becomes too powerful and oppressive. When the government controls the media, education, economy, and military, it can manipulate the people and silence dissent.

The public may not even realize that they are losing their freedoms because they are fed propaganda and lies to make them think they are living in a democracy, but they are living in a dictatorship.

What is the solution to such a situation? A robust civil society, a free press, an independent judiciary, and a vigilant citizenry can hold the government accountable and protect their rights.

Is it too late for America to return to civil society under the Constitution the founders established for us to live in freedom and justice for all?

THE LEFT OF A COUNTRY & WHAT'S LEFT, a sequel to *NARCISSISM RISING! THE FINAL WORLD EMPIRE,*

We will explore the following:

•Why Open Borders?

•How a Cabal Functions

•How Predictive Programming is sometimes used to reveal what's coming next.

•What's really behind the Climate Alarmists and their plans?

•The Infiltration of Marxism in America.

•Propaganda

•Critical Theory

•Depopulation

•Journey to Insanity

•Transforming a Country

•2030 Reset & Delusion

•Despiteful of Truth

These are just some of the topics discussed and more.

The Left of a Country & What's Left describes how ancient wisdom and prophecies continue to illuminate the path for the future and communicate, presenting the "truth" in this present day. Whether one is a seasoned student of the ancient text or an outsider, this timely message will inspire and realign us to find peace despite the upside-down world we live in.

THE LEFT OF A COUNTRY

At one time, the Left of America stood for values, social policies, and political ideas that the average person believed in. It is no longer the case as a more radical and progressive viewpoint has drastically altered the decline in those beliefs that Americans once embraced.

New Left activists emerged in the 1960s and 1970s and challenged the way of Life Americans are accustomed to, as well as those traditions and values, by introducing radical Left ideologies.

Some of those challenges during the 1960s and 1970s were toward a Cold War consensus. They advocated for participatory democracy, peace, feminism, environmentalism, and gay rights, such as Students for Democratic Society, the Women's Liberation Movement, and the Gay Liberation Front.

Liberals and Progressives who support reforms within the existing capitalist system to promote social welfare, civil liberties, human rights, and multiculturalism, such as the

New Deal Coalition, the Great Society programs, and the Democratic Party.

Within the various groups emerged a mixture of ideologies, strategies, and goals, but amongst such groups, one common vision is shared by all to support the Democrat Platform despite its radical, far-left viewpoint.

The 1960s was a decade of social and political turmoil in America, marked by the rise of the New Left, a movement of young activists who rejected their parent's political views and social and moral viewpoints of the mainstream Democratic Party.

Marxist thinkers influenced the New Left, criticizing American society and advocating for a cultural revolution.

The New Left challenged the authority of institutions such as the government and military, the media, and universities. It sought to transform them through protest demonstrations that turned violent at times.

The Left was radicalized by its disillusionment and failed to meet its demands for radical change, bringing about more radical, far-left viewpoints and ideologies.

Hillary Clinton and Barack Obama are examples of just some leaders who embraced far-left viewpoints. They were staunch followers of Saul Alinsky, who wrote the book Rules for Radicals. Saul Alinsky was a Marxist/communist and community organizer. He was skilled in stirring up resentment and frustrations in people to convey his message of a new social way for the betterment of humanity.

As the new movement of a far-left viewpoint emerged from the Leftists in America during the 1960s and 1970s, those who embraced their ideologies no longer remained activists but became extremists.

The once-Democrat party that stood for the people and its values and traditions became the New Democrat Party of Extremism.

The "Squad," four women of color elected to Congress 2018-2020, are also part of the radical Left extremist in the progressive wing of the Democrat Party and advocate extremism in their narratives.

As the Liberal Left in America became more extreme, their viewpoints became more distorted and delusional. As each stage of their delusional policies went into effect, they surpassed reality and now embraced extremism in their narratives, goals, and agendas.

How far will society continue to follow extremists in setting the precedent for the populace to live by?

America is in free fall; a decline in social, political, and moral decay has brought about oppressive and harsh policies to a once-Christian nation that is slowly losing its sovereignty.

As the Left continues to tighten the noose by introducing far-left narratives to society and met with little to no resistance, we, as a country, will become unrecognizable and extinct as a free nation and have only ourselves to blame as we choose to sit back and do nothing by handing America over to the globalist masters who are influenced by the demonic and the Left of a country will continue to dismantle what's left in a country.

{ **2** }

THE TRANSFORMATION
OF A COUNTRY

Their brief journey on a narrative used by the Obamas to unify the races and remove the racial divide in the country helped him win the White House, only to revert to a more robust method of racial division in governing the country.

After instilling anxiety in America for eight years, the Obamas left the White House and a country in total ruins, a racial divide among its people that left its impact on the hearts of so many Americans as well as anti-Christian bias.

Christian Bakers and Florist were brought to court and lost their businesses, and it was hard for parents to have a say so in the public education system, and boys were permitted to use girls' locker rooms and restrooms.

As Victor Davis Hanson reported, To advance the goals of promoting unrestricted immigration, enforcing the use of wind and solar energy, emphasizing racial differences as critical, and using the power of the government for political gain, Obama resorted to vilifying his opponents and portraying the entire country of America as lacking any distinctive qualities; police officers were terrible, people living in the mid-west had a profound lack of knowledge and harbored discrimination attitudes.

Obama's solution to all his unhappiness in the country was a comprehensive Social/Marxist overhaul as his only way of rescuing a society like America with its long history of oppression and racism.

The people finally realized the lies spoken to them and rose in revolt against such absurdity.

The hallmark of Obama's presidency was his divisive inadequacies. His only contribution was Obamacare, which effectively dismantled the entire framework of a previously functional health insurance system, undermined the revered doctor-patient connection, and eroded the ease of obtaining services from a skilled specialist.

The Obamas left the White House as billionaires living in mansions and throwing parties for their celebrity friends and Far-Left political associates. And residence in a mansion blocks away from the White House is a cause for concern.

The American Fundamental Transformation began with Obama. His mission to set up headquarters in his mansion blocks from the White House leads many to believe his transformation of America is ongoing.

The deceitful media equipped the tsunami of the Left's redesigning of America.

Although it was primarily executed in secrecy, the American people witnessed a bloodless Marxist revolution unfold by the Left. They have benefited successfully because of the lack of organized resistance and the crushing defeat of anyone who dared to challenge the power brokers in any institution.

The corruption epidemic in the nation has progressed to the point where the sole remaining political party has joined the Progressives by compromising our Constitution to enrich themselves through tactics that benefit their Marxist ideology.

American citizens who still believe in the Constitution and the Rule of law find themselves in a situation where the borders are unrestricted, the voting system is questioned, and they are unable to voice their preference regarding the form of government they desire.

The last remaining authority is the Second Amendment, which some on the far Left are also trying to eradicate.

It is impossible to call a place a nation if it does not have formal voting rights and geographical boundaries.

It is not a nation if the Rule of law does not protect its people.

A Marxist dictatorship is a country where the executive branch controls all branches of government, including the judiciary, the media, schools, and politicians.

{ **3** }

A GENERATIONAL CURSE

In 1776, 56 notable and courageous patriots signed the Declaration of Independence, who put their lives on the line, knowing they could be tried for treason and the punishment of death by hanging.

According to sources, these men were of different professions; over half were lawyers and jurists. Others were merchants and shippers who traded throughout the colonies. Some were plantation owners and farmers who owned large estates and worked the land, and others practiced medicine and were physicians who cared for the sick.

These noblemen represented different regions, religions, and interests. Still, all shared one common vision of liberty and independence for their new nation of America as they broke away from British Rule imposed upon the people, which was oppressive, with unfair taxes and policies.

The founders believed that God gave their rights and liberties to the people and that the government should respect and protect them.

All generations throughout history have followed and upheld such policies upon which this country was founded. Still, one generation rebelled against such policies and decided to do things differently. That generation is the Boomer generation.

The New Baby Boomer Generation

Never in the history of a country has any generation departed from a "Biblical World View" until the "Boomer" Generation.

The Bible tells us that in the last days, all the people's sins will fall on one generation, and we are now reaping what we have sown.

The Left in the Boomer Generation has sown:

•Taking Prayer out of the school culture.

•The Humanist Culture.

•The Divorce Culture.

•The Abortion Culture.

•The Deadbeat Dad Culture.

•The Drug Culture.

•The Radical Feminist Culture.

•The Rainbow Culture.

•The Latch-Key Kid Culture.

•The Political Correctness Culture.

•The Division of a Country Culture

•Cancel Culture.

•The Woke Culture.

•The Gender Confused Culture.

•"Truth" no longer matters, Culture.

•Calling Good Evil and Evil Good Culture.

•Anti-God Culture.

Cultural norms have shifted, so the world we once knew has become unrecognizable.

Similar to the cities of Sodom and Gomorrah in the past, the generation known as the "baby boomer" generation (1946-1964) had a sense of arrogance and indulgence due to their prosperity and leisure, which eventually drove them to engage in morally objectionable behavior.

Suppose you are a committed follower of Christ. In that case, none of the above applies to you because you are now part of God's family, and it does not matter what generation you are in because you are in covenant with God.

A Marxist/ Sexual revolution began in the 1960s, and as a result, over 62 million pregnancies in the United States ended in the termination of a newborn because of medical advancement that made "the pill" possible and legalized abortions in 1973.

The respect for authority during that era was lost, and they started calling police "pigs" and other obscenities as the "spirit of the age" became a driving force in many of the young people.

In the 1970s, many of the new generation started to assume leadership positions in the workforce.

As time passed, the new message in places like companies, businesses, schools, colleges, and the pulpits grew increasingly secular and more to the far left as they disconnected from Godly principles and scripture.

Over time, what was considered abnormal and lawless gradually became socially acceptable.

The "baby boomers" generation of the radical- far-left, who normalized what God calls sin, "set" the precedent for the younger generations in America to follow and are now reaping what they have sown as the generational curse has engulfed not only America but the world.

Furthermore, there is no stopping the degradation and madness that America is experiencing because of the "sins of the fathers" we now witness, unless by divine intervention and if God destroyed ancient civilizations for rebellion against His direction and principles, what makes this generation so different?

God's Word has been replaced by science and human knowledge and reasoning, which is precisely why the flood destroyed every human being except Noah and his family. The Tower of Babel Builders, Lot's Day, and many other significant illustrations in the Bible reference God rejecting generations of people for turning against Him and serving idols in that era.

The idols in America are so numerous that it is impossible to name them all.

(Romans 1) in the Bible is a good illustration of a "generational curse" because God allows individuals to have what they want after so many attempts to steer them in the right direction. They refuse, so God gives them over to what He calls "a reprobate mind'; in other words, He allows them to have what they want even though He says no, and that is a dangerous place to be.

Adequate reverence for God's Word has declined as "truth" is no longer recognized.

Those who still hold to "truth" and biblical beliefs are scoffed at and rejected and considered deplorable and a threat to society.

Hollywood and corporate media spread disinformation about those who stand for "truth" in a society that is broken down because of madness and unrealistic ideologies brought on by the "spirit of the age" in an upside-down world.

Seasons of difficulties are upon those devoted followers of the gospel of Christ. The departure of those who remained faithful, who have passed on and gone to heaven, is now being replaced by a new generation of individuals who have no regard for the things of God, and their foolish hearts are darkened.

However, this country's "spirit of the age" displays a generational curse upon America for the fathers' sins, and it is now reaping what it has sown.

The "spirit of the age" is the world system everyone is born under in this world, which is ruled, as the Bible tells us, by Satan.

The far-left and their supporters in the "Baby Boomer" generation in America just flat-out walked away from all principles, virtues, and the Rule of God and nature's law that the Creator set before us to live by. As a result, the younger generations grow up without biblical knowledge or a moral compass to guide them. Now, it appears a "Generational Curse" is over America and the world, and because this country is so steeped in "sin," the Creator has removed His hand of blessing He once had on this country.

{ **4** }

OPEN BORDERS

The Left in the country comprises progressives, far-left, liberals, and the Democrat party; all support and agree to what is termed The Great Reset, which is Agenda 2030, an established Global Government in which unelected wealthy bureaucrats will rule over the lower-class, serfs.

2009 was the start of the transformation in the country, and in 2016, America was given a short reprieve until 2020; from then on, we have witnessed the dismantling of a once great nation.

Open borders are being utilized to transform the sovereignty of a capitalistic society.

The global elite is anti-American and cannot have their "new order" as long as America remains a superpower and keeps its sovereignty.

The country's massive transformation still has more to follow.

Destroying the framework America is built upon is the call for the Great Reset. The slogan "Build Back Better" fits that description of what is transpiring in America. Still, it is not "Build Back Better" for society; it is meant to fulfill their utopian dream of greed, power, and pleasure with only two groups of people: the Global Elite and the serfs.

Open Borders is a disaster for an already overpopulated country where millions of people have already flooded into the United States of America.

Driven by an astronomical number of people pouring into the country daily, the global elite are on a fast track to dismantle a country that is not only trillions of dollars in debt but also, as mentioned, eradicating American sovereignty.

The U.N. long ago desired all nations to be borderless, and as we witnessed in Europe in 2015, the power brokers have removed America's borders; as a result, millions more can flood into the country, and their plan for a "new order" of world government will be achieved.

During the Biden years, radical border policies, according to the House Committee on Oversight and Accountability Chairman, discussed that the regime is fueling unprecedented illegal immigration and jeopardizing security at our borders.

Furthermore, efforts to undermine Immigration law continue to run rampant by the regime, and a deterrent to the danger of the uncontrolled southern border looks grim.

Border patrols are overwhelmed with thousands of illegals entering the country daily as American citizens are no longer protected, as the administration disregards the danger of a difficult situation and is not enforcing the law.

The only thing being done by the Biden administration

is to provide funds to the border to process illegals faster so they can be released into the country.

Since 2020, the crisis at the border has become a humanitarian catastrophe and a peril to national security.

Those crossing the border into the country are not coming to assimilate but to congregate.

In crossing the border, authorities have detained thousands of migrant children traveling alone, and hundreds have perished.

The enduring consequences of the administration's inability to maintain control over the southern border are detrimental to national sovereignty and pose a significant risk, as sovereignty is fundamental to American security.

Obama's last White House Correspondents Dinner on April 30, 2016, scoffed as he said, "The End of the Republic has never looked better."

Have you ever heard a leader of a country say such a thing?

As the Leftist hierarchy continues the radical transformation of America, everyone else, no matter race, profession, religion, or political party one adheres to, will experience the hardships and struggles as "serfs" serving the Global Conglomerates.

{ 5 }

A CABAL

A "Cabal" is an organization engaged in a covert scheme or conspiracy. Additionally, the term may pertain to the conspiracy per se or the clandestine organization that executes the plot.

A conspiracy of left-wing extremists can plot together a plan they so desire and use the media food chain of radical left-wing activists, who are not news reporters, as its origin and mainstream news outlets as its destination to condition the public by using false information.

Once the narrative flows through the mainstream media, the public believes it to be valuable information and never questions what they are told despite any adverse effects projected upon them.

Hollywood is another excellent example of pushing such information upon the public, convincing them that what they hear is accurate and reliable, as most celebrities embrace a liberal left-wing agenda. Those actors that don't go along with the false narrative are ostracized.

A conspiracy strengthens and gains more ground for its nefarious plot as all facets of society accept the narrative presented by the media, Hollywood, academia, and others, and the propaganda is distributed throughout society.

Covid 19 is an example of a "cabal" using experimentation on the world and vaccines that are harmful to the immune system, as many scientists and medical professionals have proven.

Fear is a tactic a "cabal" will use on the population of the world for them to use a "medical treatment" because the people trust what they have been told to be accurate information.

Consider, if you will, a group of individuals who monitor speech in the country as part of a cabal of liberal left elites who advocate keeping tabs on public discussions in the United States, particularly that of prominent politicians and the Hollywood elite.

Departure from the liberal playbook exposes one to the possibility of facing public retaliation.

It is left-wing media outlets, corrupt politicians, some in the entertainment industry, and others who have a consistent pattern of using disinformation to ostracize anyone of dissent. Yet, the blatant hypocrisy used as they "spin" the narrative, accusing others of doing the very thing they do, is absurd.

Furthermore, far-left extremism is advocated in their policies and agendas.

It is best to understand that some influential, wealthy individuals have chosen to be involved in a scheme of oppressive ideologies that usher in their New World Order of global governance.

We have witnessed in the country how homelessness in the streets is a national concern, as well as Veterans being thrown out of facilities to be replaced as shelters for migrants.

Still, we have now reached a point where those on the left side of the spectrum are not concerned with public opinion, the welfare of American citizens, freedom of speech, and safety concerns regarding the borders as fentanyl and other drugs are pouring into the country, human trafficking, children are sold into sex trafficking, terrorist entering the country, and gangs controlling the borders.

The Social Compact is Broken:

A social compact is when the community silently agrees to strive for the greater good with mutual respect and trust in each other and the institutions that uphold the Rule of law.

When the Social Compact is broken, people lose faith in the system and each other and become more selfish, violent, and opportunistic.

It credits a fertile ground for criminals to exploit the weaknesses and vulnerabilities of society, and criminals can take control of the lack of social cohesion, the erosion of moral values, and the absence of effective law enforcement.

They can undermine the country's security, stability, and prosperity. Therefore, it is vital to maintain and strengthen the social compact to prevent the government from being overrun by criminals.

A cabal can break the Social Compact of society and gain control over a country by using various methods, such as:

•Spreading misinformation and using it on the people as propaganda to manipulate public opinion creates division and distrust among different groups.

•Infiltrating and corrupting key institutions and organizations such as the media, the judiciary, the military, intelligence agencies, and political parties.

•Recruiting and bribing influential individuals who can advance their agendas and sabotage their opponents.

•Orchestrating false flag operations and crises to create chaos and fear and justify authoritarian measures and interventions.

•They are eliminating or silencing anyone who opposes or exposes them, such as whistleblowers, journalists, activists, and dissidents.

By doing these things, a plot can undermine the existing government's and society's legitimacy and authority, erode the values and norms that bind people, and create a power vacuum they can fill with their puppet regime or ideology.

Consider if values and norms that once bonded this country together erode, and media that are activists putting out disinformation to fit a narrative, celebrities, a broken education system that once was a "learning center" but now indoctrinating centers, teachings that go against the principles of God and natures law, and Marxist ideologies.

Ivy League universities have become overrun by Socialist/Marxist professors teaching students that capitalism is wrong, and as a result, protesting in the streets of America, at times, has become violent as more division and erosion of values and norms continue to destroy what's left of a country.

{ **6** }

JOURNEY TO INSANITY

The Apostle Paul prophesied to forewarn those who will listen about what to expect in this generation, which can be summed up in (2 Timothy 12-13). All those who live according to God's Word will suffer persecution, and wicked and evil individuals will become more deceiving and grow worse.

(Romans 1:28-32) It reveals why evil continues and what the result is. It explains how people rebel against the principles God sets before us to live by. After God has used all matters of trying to reach them, they continually reject His "truths," He then turns them over to a "reprobate mindset' to do those things God says 'No" to, knowing they will be judged, and enjoy doing them regardless of the punishment. Please make no mistake; it is precisely what we are eye-witnesses to in America.

We are beholding the insanity that has resulted from humanity's abandonment of God and choosing to do what they desire in their perverse thinking.

Those who are not in a state of being united with Christ

by repenting of their sins and asking Him into their Life have succumbed to the influence of the "spirit of the age" (Satan), who initiated the presence of sin inside the human genetic makeup.

The influence referred to is responsible for infection, influencing sin into the mass of humanity with a "depraved mindset" characterized by distorted thinking that is contrary to the mentality of those who are committed Christ followers who are redeemed, which leads to the manifestation of morally upright actions that are found only through Jesus.

We are eyewitnesses to the things unraveling the fundamental structure of Western civilization as insanity erodes our usual way of Life. Those signs show us plainly what we are dealing with in a country.

The economy, social unrest, and politics have become volatile for an extended period.

True evil emerges as political conflict and economic collapse wreak havoc on cultural systems.

Initially, the events were gradual, but eventually, they happened abruptly and were completed.

The increasing predominance of Narcissistic individuals who have reached the point of insanity and display abnormal behavior in public is a "red alert" of impending doom and collapse in Western civilization.

As wealthy hierarchy individuals in a country have reached an insanity level, they begin to feel free to indulge in their most destructive urges without facing any accountability for their actions and harm to a country and its people.

When an individual is without a moral compass, it affects their daily thinking.

An excellent example of far-leftist thinking:

•Men can give birth to babies.

•Parents who are outraged at their children's public school system that sponsors drag queen performances to 7-year-olds are haters and considered transphobic.

•They are unable to identify what a woman is.

•Individuals are xenophobic if they don't want millions of people to illegally enter the country by putting up a barrier of barbed wire or a wall.

•Cities, suburbs, and towns are safer without police protection.

•You are anti-science if you don't believe in a climate emergency.

•It is okay for young children to have their body parts mutilated.

At this time, we are seeing the results of what Jesus and the prophets forewarned about in this generation, and it is increasingly apparent to those who study biblical prophecy those things we are witnessing.

Once the insanity has reached its ultimate destructive level, God will then intervene in the affairs of all wicked and perverse individuals by pouring out His Wrath upon unregenerated people living on Planet Earth.

The only thing holding back His judgment at this time, the Rapture of His church, must first occur. After that, His Judgments fall on insane individuals who have chosen to

receive a "reprobate mind (insanity) instead of the acknowl-
edgment of "truth" found only in Jesus Christ.

THE WAR ON CHRISTIANITY

The far left in America is not only united in the removal of traditions, values, virtues, and what God calls good, but all of Christendom as well.

The origin of the anti-Christian crusade in America goes back to Communism.

Following the downfall of the Communist empire, liberals were unwilling to surrender their idealistic and atheistic beliefs. As a result, they opted to remake their vision and now refer to their cause as "Social Justice" and no longer use the term" Communism."

Liberals are willing to resort to any tactics to silence those who oppose their anti-Christian views. Their crusade against Christianity was an attack on the United States of America itself.

Why did President Biden declare Easter Sunday, March 31, 2024, "Transgender Day"?

Why is Biden's DOJ going after several people in Tennessee for praying peacefully in the street outside an Abortion clinic and facing a possible "Life sentence" in prison?

Why did Jill Biden declare that the White House Easter Egg hunt of March 31, 2024, will not allow a Christian theme in the Easter egg art decoration contest?

It has been a White House tradition to allow children to decorate Easter eggs with a Christian theme, and Biden's decided they will no longer allow it.

Why did Biden's Department of Education "pledge" he would shut down America's most prominent Christian University?

Remember when we were told "Merry Christmas" was politically incorrect?

I could go on, but I hope you can now see what side of the political spectrum has chosen to reject Godly principles and standards.

Over the past few years, the well-known and prominent Archbishop Vigano has composed a series of eloquent letters concerning the biblical-like global formation of two opposing factions: The children of darkness and the children of light.

The children of light are the most prominent segment of society, while the children of darkness are a small minority. However, the former group's experience of prejudice categorizes them as deficient compared to their opponents.

Individuals with hostile intentions frequently accept influential roles within the government, economy, political spectrum, and media.

The manifestation of the children of darkness is a dangerous and mindful force to be dealt with, and they perceive Christianity as their adversary and a significant hindrance to the acceptance of their core beliefs, which are vital to their goals for authority and dominance.

It is a war to destroy Christianity as the darkness manifests in human individuals to oppose, reject, oppress, and suppress anyone who has a biblical worldview.

The offspring of darkness's belief that Christianity must perish is the source of their war on believers.

A succession of historical decisions by the Supreme Court in 1962 eventually prohibited the teaching of religion in public schools and abolished the mention of God altogether.

Madlyn Murray, Christopher Hitchen, Margaret Sanger, and various other liberal leftists played significant roles in challenging societal norms, influencing the legal ruling on religious freedom, same-sex marriage, and abortions, and the author of Life, Jesus was forsaken by the Democrat Party that once declared, In God We Trust.

At present, America now has a base in the left party that serves as a (war) on Christianity, as the assaults on the founding principles of religious liberty and equality are shattered using smear campaigns and labeling people who hold to their faith as bigots.

The liberal Left uses as their tool the education system and media to spread their hate and propaganda to influence their listeners with assaults on Christianity.

Sexism, racism, and social justice are all terms and tools

used to justify their cause in the tearing down of Christianity in America.

Hollywood and other companies as well as play a significant role in tearing down any Christian principles and methods left in America.

The forces of darkness operate within a liberal party to delegitimize and dehumanize anyone who holds to the Truth and takes a stand for reality and righteousness.

Never before in the history of this country have we seen the manifestation of extreme hatred coming from the Left toward God and His design for humanity to live by.

They were arresting several people for praying silently in front of an abortion clinic who are now facing 11 years in prison.

It's acceptable, however, to install a statue of Baphomet in the Iowa state capital. Baphomet is a deity used in ancient times to sacrifice their children.

Satan after school clubs and Satan worship is acceptable behavior thanks to the liberal Left in America but dare not mention Jesus in the public square because it is all part of a communist plan used to remove capitalism in America and usher in the Left's dream of a Marxist/ Social state.

The "truth" does not rest in the hearts of modern-life liberals in society today. Instead, they have a spiritual appetite for idolatry and self-indulgence.

The human will of the idolaters on the Left is a pious attitude that they proclaim not to judge anyone for their behavior except those who hold to a "biblical worldview. "

It does not matter to those on the left side of the spectrum that they live a "lie" because their master, Satan, is the father of Lies, and for this cause, they do what they do.

They disguise their lies so the reality of their lies can be ignored by society.

Christians are on a journey in a strange land. As the foundations continue to crumble all around us in our journey, it is essential to remember what our Savior told His disciples, "If they persecuted Him, all those who follow Him would suffer persecution," as well.

PREARRANGED SCHEMING

Many reports have surfaced that elite globalists use predictive programming to ensure that the public does not react adversely or unexpectedly in events or situations that are not everyday occurrences.

It is done by discreetly hinting at its intended upcoming developments in popular movies and other media so that the public is psychologically prepared and open to social change when it finally occurs.

Some individuals believe it is a subtle method of psychological conditioning used in entertainment, movies, and other methods to enlighten the public with the organized upcoming changes in society carried out by the progressive leftists.

Once the new changes in society take place, they hope that the public will have already been conditioned by the predictions, and by doing so, an adverse reaction will be dismissed, and changes will seem normal.

Additionally, some say liberals use this method to ensure that the public will continue to have faith in the present system of governance; others report elite liberals will organize an event and then send out hints in movies and other media so that when the event is released, the public will rely on the ruling class with more than the expected reliance because of fear of what has occurred; despite a volatile situation such as Covid-19.

The movie "Contagion" portrayed scenarios reminiscent of COVID-19 roughly nine years before its appearance and global spread.

Furthermore, the movie The Simsons in 1999 exhibited an episode called "The City of New York vs. Homer Simpson, which resembles numerous aspects of the 9/11 disaster.

Another movie, "Bird Flu," produced in 2006, depicts a pandemic of avian flu (bird flu) that transforms into a human-transmitted virus is the setting of this movie. An American businessman contacts the fatal mutant bird flu virus while in China and returns to the USA via airplane. Millions die after it spreads from human to human.

The N.Y. Post reported on February 15, 2024, that using "strains of avian influenza virus" that pose the most significant risk to the human population, the Biden administration will spend $1 million taxpayer dollars from April 2021 to March 2026 on "wet lab virology studies" in the Wuhan lab in China, the same lab from which COVID-19 was released.

On April 3, 2024, the largest U.S. egg-producing plant in

the country, located in Texas, had to close because bird flu was detected.

The plant had to kill 1.6 million hens and 337,000 young ones with the virus.

It is eerily like the arsonist burning down many of the giant chicken farms throughout the country over the past couple of years.

Many additional incidents appear to foreshadow subsequent events about high tech and knowledge.

Another movie, "Apocalypse 11 Revelation," released in 1999, depicts after the Rapture, Christians are hated and hunted down. The "haters" (Christians) formed an underground resistance movement and are forced into a time-sensitive situation, as the world government supplies "Virtual Reality" headsets to each individual living on planet Earth to be enabled on the "Day of Wonders."

Sources have reported how a planned-out crisis is released into society. Then the government comes forth with a solution to that problem, knowing years in advance and at the right time, once the plot is delivered in predictive programming, intentionally postponing applying the answer until it would inflict the most significant possible harm on people's capacity for independent thought so that once again, people depend on the government (a form of fear).

Is predictive programming a proper term to use as an idea in movies, books, and broadcasting to familiarize the public with upcoming events?

Obama's movie, "Leave the World Behind," is the latest "buzz" on social media about predictive programming.

It is a movie about how the world will crumble if the power grid is turned off, and millions of people will die in such a disaster.

Watching the movie is an eye-opener, and you should be frightened after watching it as it portrays how approximately 90 percent of the population in the United States is projected to perish within the first year if the power grid goes down.

Obama is the film's producer and significantly influenced the script to portray the movie as realistically achievable.

How they communicate and develop the story paints a picture of how civilization would respond to an upcoming disaster, perhaps (leaders' views), to anticipate and support particular acts and results.

Other reports have surfaced that with 2024 being an Election year, and such unsettlement and division in the country, predictive programming in the movie is a cause for concern.

With the invasion at the border and the globalist puppets in politics ensuring that their agenda will become a reality, anything is possible.

{ **9** }

INFRASTRUCTURE

The liberal Left has supported and allowed the invasion at the border, and as a result, our infrastructure is in danger to those who want to cause havoc to us.

Hackers can cause serious harm to the "water systems" of a country by disrupting the water supply, quality, and safety.

A good example is that hackers can tamper with the sensors, valves, pumps, and controllers that regulate the water flow and pressure, resulting in water shortages, leaks, floods, or contamination.

Hackers can also access the data and records of the water systems, such as customer information, billing details, and operation logs, and profound results can occur by compromising the privacy and safety of the water system's operations.

Hackers can also use the water system as a gateway to attack other critical infrastructure, such as the power grid, transportation networks, or health facilities, causing widespread damage and disruption to society and the economy.

Therefore, it is vital to protect water systems from cyberattacks and to ensure their reliability.

In 2020, a hacker tried to poison the water supply of a Florida city by increasing the sodium hydroxide level in the water treatment plant.

In 2015, a hacker breached the network of a water company in Israel and attempted to change the chlorine levels in the water.

In May 2023, U.S. Microsoft warned that Chinese hackers were attacking critical infrastructure. Christopher Wray, FBI director, on February 4, 2024, announced that the Chinese may be attacking America's critical infrastructure because 2024 is an Election year.

On April 18, 2024, the FBI alerted the public that the Chinese were preparing to attack U.S. Infrastructure.

We are hearing the alarms and warning bells ahead of time and how convenient it is for America's enemies, being an Election year!

Next, Gov reported experts told the House Subcommittee we were vulnerable to hackers attacking the power grid.

National Security Advisor Jake Sullivan and Environmental Protection Agency Administrator Michael Regan issued a cautionary statement, highlighting the occurrence of debilitating cyberattacks targeting water and wastewater infrastructure across the United States.

Could we have witnessed "predictive programming" in such a fragile situation?

Time will tell what may occur, and we should remember Obama's movie, "Leave the World Behind."

If an emergency were to break out, whoever was running the country could declare a state of emergency and enforce martial law, and that person could remain in power indefinitely.

We have been warned of the possibility of an attack on our infrastructure, and with 2024 being an election year, we should take it very seriously.

If we are watching in "real-time" the Left's prediction for America, then it is not hard for us to contemplate what will occur as they usher in their 2030 Reset Agenda.

LIARS

In 2024 A.D., we find ourselves in a position that is precisely at the end of the "church age" on Planet Earth.

The wicked and deceitful who create false information are hostile toward God and His people and anything good. The lies are never-ending, as the righteous are assaulted through liberal social media, podcasts, T.V. networks, and entertainment. The scriptures reveal that Lucifer is called "The father of lies" by Jesus Himself as He taught His disciples, and the devil is cunning and possesses the skill of "crat" when he delivers a deceptive narrative to his followers, ensuring the effectiveness of the deception that frequently appears as genuine.

A good example:

Medical professionals and researchers who are not beholden to or financially supported by a global organization such as the WHO, WEF, the Davos Club, or Big Pharma have proven that the COVID-19 shots are unsafe; despite that, big pharma persists in spreading deceit and refers to the substances as effective and safe.

The greedy, self-serving mass industry, like its master Lucifer, possesses excellent skill in crafting deceit by deliberately employing sincere, friendly, yet unsuspecting individuals in its advertisements.

It merely illustrates the understated deception and nature of the striking resemblance of the "liars" to their origin.

Satan, as identified by Jesus, has transformed lying into a refined and elaborate art.

Please pay attention to any anti-christian organization such as the World Health Organization, World Economic Forum, the United Nations, and young global leaders who have received training from Klaus Schwab, and any dishonest, morally compromised politicians from various political parties across the globe in addition to the media outlets controlled by globalist entities, what their narrative is they are promoting.

The fundamental goals of Klaus Schwab and the World Economist Forum for Global Governance have only been made public in the last several years.

Their plan to establish a Marxist totalitarian, global government- "Build Back Better" was a cover for the actual goal of enslaving the entire planet and is being publicly discussed in private meetings that they now welcome the news media to attend.

Please pay attention to information regarding climate change, the state of the economy, the invasion at the border, the statistics on poll numbers, the identification of who the real criminals are and whom they portray to be heroic and moral individuals, as well as their enemies of politics, and anyone who disagrees with their fabricated narratives.

Narcissistic individuals continue to engage in falsehoods, while others genuinely convince themselves that their lies are accurate.

The most astounding thing is that some individuals who are elite politicians, despite having lied repeatedly over many years and told scores of falsehoods of various sizes, nobody seems to notice, and there is no resistance to their lies.

Even though many of the lying politicians of the D.C. swamp have been exposed, their loyal followers could care less that they are being lied to; shake it off and continue to support the radical extremist.

The D.C. swamp and others believe that most, if not everyone, can be deceived each time they speak.

It is possible for any individual who is a habitual liar, irrespective of their financial position, race, or ethnic background, to claim Satan as their father because he is their influencer, and they gladly accept the "task" he delivers to that person.

All liars who continue in their skill at lying will share their fate in the same place the father of lies winds up for eternity.

Lying is used to transform a once-free country into a Marxist/Communist statehood and advance its agenda into a highly hostile world of deception, idolatry, and pervasive immorality.

As long as the "normal" people turn the other way, submit

to the lies and distortions presented to them, and offer their children up to Molech because of the "lies" told to them, their fate will be a rude awakening. It is how the Left in a country control what's left in a country.

{ 11 }

THE PLAYBOOK

Understanding how the far-leftist operates starts with liberal billionaires such as George Soros, who funds many leftist organizations and discredits anyone who challenges the progressive narrative and who has a conservative voice.

They plan a strategy and then deliver it to various Leftist organizations to promote their agenda.

Reports have revealed how they influence every government, judicial system, education, medical, entertainment, and more.

The liberal playbook is controlled by shady operatives that use the media to release their fake news on whatever they desire; they spread the dirt on their political opponents, patriots, conservatives, Christians, and anyone with an opposing view.

When they do so, they exert influence over the information the public is exposed to and how society forms its opinions and decisions made during voting.

The narrative in their playbook is exaggerated, scandalous, and harmful, and they use it to influence public opinion.

Public smears are nothing new in America.

During the initial stages of the formation of the United States, Thomas Jefferson openly announced Alexander Hamilton's involvement in an extramarital relationship with Maria Reynolds. In response, Hamilton criticized Jefferson for his relationship with his enslaved individual, Sally Hemings.

However, the advancement of technology in the 21st century, namely the emergence of social media, has elevated the practice of political disinformation efforts to unprecedented heights.

The credibility of the traditional media took a hit during the 2016 election due to the apparent bias displayed by presumably trustworthy news organizations.

The liberals no longer need corporate media in many of their smear campaigns against their specific targets; according to sources, many individuals get news information from social media, Facebook, X, and other alternative news sites.

Facebook scans individuals using algorithms to censor anyone with a conservative voice and to "weaponize" their political opponents.

A steady flow of misinformation is then sent out to the public using smears and other methods to criticize any individual who opposes the liberal ideology, and the reproach of it all is that they spin the narrative and claim to be overseers of society and as they always use the term; for the good of the democracy.

The United States is a republic and not a democracy. The difference between the two and why they always use the term democracy is that in a democracy, they divide the people into "groups."

In a "republic," people have "individual rights" and are not put into "groups" such as race, ethnic background, or religious beliefs.

It is why Obama said during his speech at his last correspondence dinner at the White House, "The Downfall of the Republic never looked better." Obama knew back then what the plan was in the liberal playbook, and we have witnessed their atrocities come to pass; the "Downfall of the Republic" continues at a steady flow and will one day come to an end as long as we continue to follow the same pattern by the Left we are on now.

Contributions to the Leftist playbook is a whopping chest of financial resources ready to be distributed as needed, and in that playbook are organizations that employ a large number of opposition researchers and allocate their significant resources, aiming to undermine prominent conservatives to delegitimize any conservative movement.

While the organizations may not directly initiate the smears and controversies leading to conservatives' downfall, they invest significant amounts of money in investigating and scrutinizing them thoroughly.

Furthermore, the organizations exhibit zero tolerance toward (diversity of opinion) and defame and discredit any individual who expresses ideas aligned with the right of the political spectrum.

The Liberal Playbook is also used by allocating diversity and other "terms" as an outlet for pushing their left-wing agenda, and the "diversity" term they use is one-sided, meaning their liberal diversity.

The Liberal Playbook is a left-wing set of beliefs, terms, and ideologies used to fit the narrative they need at any specific time, and there is no tolerance for any opposing view.

Examples of some terms used:

•Xenophobe

•Bigot

•Fascist

•Deplorables

•White privilege

•Mega lovers

•Racist

The Left hates the term "Make America Great Again." Have you ever given serious thought as to why someone does not want the country they live in to be great? It should be seriously considered, and to ignore it probably means the individual who feels this way is unhappy in their country and, perhaps, should find a happier place to live. It's just that simple.

The liberal agenda is a Marxist/Communist plot to remove all traces of capitalism and the sovereignty of the country and enslave every individual by issuing a digital I.D., digital passport, and digital currency to benefit the elite power holders to be the guardians of the Earth and Rule by

way of an "authoritarian regime" in a one-world -government and anyone who resists their Utopia will be punished.

Marxism and Movements

Marxism is a comprehensive theory encompassing society, economics, and politics, and many of the large-scale campaigns in the United States originate from a Marxist ideology. Such campaigns are the framework of a utopia, alluring to people because they are at the core of specific declarations of a transcendental future and the capability of individuals to become perfect.

But before such a utopia is established, the present Culture must be relinquished, and then the person can fully commit to the cause if they give up more of their independence, autonomy, etc. It is how large interest groups work.

Whatever crusade one belongs to, they are brainwashed by the destruction of one's individuality and sense of self-worth by blending them into the population while simultaneously classifying them according to factions such as money, race, age, etc., to highlight social class differences. It is how the agitators push their message publicly on behalf of the welfare and happiness of the people. At the same time, separate one from another, as a result, blindside them in different directions to dismantle the current Culture and to establish domination over the emerging one.

Those attracted to such factions in the Culture are unhappy, unsatisfied with their lives, and unable to assume accountability for wrongdoings. Blaming others, or the present system, is how they justify themselves for the wrong measures they take.

The promise of a utopian revolution and the condemnation of the current Culture, to which they have fragile or no ties, entice them. Belittling others becomes an effective strategy for discrediting individuals who have achieved success and are happy. Everyone should be on the same plane, despite their achievements, which is their narrative.

Manipulating people's fragile natures and grievances is a tool to give the person a sense of assurance and dignity; otherwise, they remain discouraged and dissatisfied.

Black Lives Matter (BLM) and Antifa are examples of large-scale campaigns with Marxist ties originating in the United States, Marxist Feminism, Revolutionaries, Trans-Marxism, and other associated groups.

Under the guise of Social Justice, Marxists in the country aim to demolish the core principles of the republic by revising history, reinstating racism, establishing privileged groups, and controlling public conversations and opinions, the armed forces, and places of religious gatherings.

The goal of the Marxists in the United States is to enslave the American people into an ideology that destroys their very core identity.

To take over North American and European economies and societies, the elite use the "Great Narrative" campaign, banking on the West's decline of conventional values and cutting-edge technology, such as Robotics, Metaverse, AI, and more, to achieve their goal.

Those in power behind these plans want to change the people of planet Earth's conceptions of "free will" and humanity itself and intend to do it globally. All one has to do is listen to Yuval Noah Harari, Klaus Schwab's close advisor to the World Economic Forum. Harari's YouTube channel exposes a lot on the subject.

The liberal elite claim that their Utopia will be complete by the year 2030 as the planet will undergo a dramatic change by that year.

Hum anocracy.

Klaus Schwab, the president of the WEF, has recently unveiled his intentions to establish a "new world" that will facilitate humanity's transition into a new century.

At the World Government Summit in Dubai, Schwab introduced his proposals for a concept he calls "hum anocracy," emphasizing globalization ideals.

The world was stunned by the announcement he declared that a new paradigm of human-centric governance was emerging. His vision of "hum anocracy" promotes a new era of industrialization that combines human existence's physical, digital, and biological dimensions.

He warned that the Fourth Industrial Revolution was uncertain, including moral issues, social inequalities, and environmental degradation.

He called upon government leaders to engage their populations.

Many scholars, including myself, have written about the bizarre plans the WEF has presented in the past; now, they are openly telling us, and it is no longer a secret.

We are thoroughly dystopian now in the West, and they play everybody for fools. The elite have elevated themselves to "godhead" status.

As mentioned, during the 1960s, the "boomer generation"

of students was receptive to insurrection. The campaign movement known as the "New Left" was born. Their universities supported radical students as they transitioned into adulthood and became professors, creating an environment where they could influence future generations.

Cultural Marxism has flooded academia to the point that public schools and universities have indoctrinated youth into a concept of theories that subsequently erode the American structure upon which the country was founded.

Youth are taught "group thinking," not individual thinking. They are not educated about the equality of all individuals; they are taught instead about racial privilege resulting from systematic racism.

They are not educated on the fact that individuals have succeeded because, in the United States, an open marketplace and freedom of ownership is the background of society, more than in any other country in the world.

They don't learn that the notion of universal human equality, which the founders fought for, has persisted through many generations. They are instead imbued with the idea that "white supremacy," not only the detestable concept of "white supremacy," but all Western traditions, relationships, customs, structures, and rules, is fundamentally racist and that the laws of the United States were meant to preserve it.

Parents Seeing Children's Indoctrination

Many parents in America today are feeling the ramifications of their children's indoctrination into a Marxist ideology in schools and universities; sadly, they are the ones funding the system through taxes, and others are paying thousands of dollars, sending their youth to private schools and universities where they to are groomed in a Marxist concept.

The majority of parents are engaged in their children's exposure to media that promotes anti-American, unrealistic, and contradictory views. The media includes books, entertainment, cartoons, video games, networking sites, web searches, and iPhone news apps.

If Marxist ideology is not overcome, modern-day Marxists may enslave America in an authoritarian ideology that destroys the soul of each individual unless they are once again destroyed.

Critical Theory & Cultural Marxism

Herbert Marcuse is German-born and the originator of the development of Critical theory, of which many large-scale campaigns developed, some being racial and gender. (CRT) Critical Race theory has been extensively covered in media.

Furthermore, it becomes complicated when it disregards not just the racial advancements achieved over many decades but also the inspiring principles of individual initiative and freedom of opportunity upon which this nation was established.

A rising philosophy of Cultural Marxism underlies the discussion over race. Proponents of Cultural Marxism are using race instead of class as the foundation for political revolution to address perceived inequalities, aiming to manipulate racial past to influence constitutional discussion, educate students in a biased manner, and pressure institutions in a manner that goes against American values and civic harmony.

Cultural Marxism teaches that absolute Truth does not exist, and it is why most followers of this ideology are atheists.

Cultural Marxism seeks to alter and reconstruct present-day society, and the ideology emphasizes transforming the Culture to be more forward-thinking and progressive.

Anti-Christian

Cultural Marxism teachings are incompatible with a biblical perspective. Beliefs such as denying objective Truth, harboring hatred toward others, and anti-Semitism are contradictory to a Christian existence.

Cultural Marxism questions the holy teachings in the Bible. It advocates for goals contrary to its principles and can mislead and deceive individuals into adopting incorrect views.

Furthermore, it is a complex ideology characterized by anti-Christian values and principles, which should be avoided if one is a believer in Christ and follows His teachings.

Karl Marx's goal was to impose a polluted alternative to a biblical worldview and to "overthrow God" and dismantle capitalism.

In a Marxist view, the church and family stand in the way of Utopia.

Marxist supporters in America are in many political leadership roles and have worked hard at ushering the dream of a Marxist state into American society.

As you can see, Christianity is not accepted in a world

run by those in leadership who have succumbed to a Marxist belief system.

Christian beliefs are entirely contrary to Karl Marx's theory, and it is why 'hate" toward believers in America has increased dramatically; nevertheless, to the faithful, there is nothing new under the sun because God and those genuinely committed to Him have been rejected from the beginning of time, and it is why Jesus Himself said, "If they have hated Him, they will hate us as well.

{ 12 }

CLIMATE CHANGE

Another concept used in the destruction of a country is Climate Change, and Marxism can be advanced through the exploitation of Climate alarmism.

Their tool is to create a narrative to appear as if there is a feeling of disaster so that the general population is compelled to trust in whatever government efforts are presented to safeguard the planet's health, even if it means slaughtering all the farm animals, energy, replacing food with GMOs, synthetic lab-grown meat, and crickets and mealworms for protein.

It is likely to result in a choice for "unified control," a trend often connected to Marxist ideology.

Climate alarmists frequently stoked anxieties about sustainability issues to advance an alternative for living and utilization, which is another goal Marxism wants to accomplish.

In his book, Facing Global Environmental Change, HG

Brauch contends that the forces of Climate change advocate radical alterations in social organizations.

The study sheds light on how Marxism has advanced through the use of climatologists.

According to Marxist theory, the privileged few take from the Earth for their benefit, and resources in the world are unfairly divided among humanity. Thus, those who adhere to a Marxist concept believe Climate change is a method to advance their differences to a system responsible for an already crisis in the environment.

Once again, Marxism is being advanced by the Climate change alarmists using fearmongering. Corrupt governments and scientists use "fear" to brainwash humanity into thinking there is a real problem with the weather.

There is no proof of the climatologist's claims, and it does not stand up to investigation.

They repeatedly emphasize that the warming of the climate leads to an increase in sea levels.

Despite numerous decades of forecasting, we are still in the same situation. The supposed source of this increase in sea levels is the melting of glaciers as if ever-huge icebergs are plummeting aimlessly across the sea.

The climate alarmists use "fear" as a weapon about food production; could it be that the worldwide baking chain has plotted to fix prices?

Greggs accounts for many food sales in the nation.

Regarding the potential mass extinctions, nothing proves it to be climate-related. Cynical scientists selectively choose deceptively.

Numerous animal species have become extinct, but it is a natural occurrence. Should we also be held accountable for the extinction of the dinosaurs?

According to a U.N. assessment, the most significant danger to the environment, forests, and animals comes from the fast-expanding cattle herds, acid rain, alien species arrival, desert formation, ocean dead zones, contamination of waterway, reef and marine life, destruction and an enormous number of other environmental crimes, are all allegedly they're doing.

They want to remove all livestock to secure their current worldwide domination.

Keep in mind the many chicken factories that burned down, and we are told arsonists are responsible for it.

Next is the extreme weather issue.

I have not noticed any variations from the typical weather patterns. Perhaps the true intentions of deceitful scientists about weather concerns are a push for wind power usage. By doing so, the globalists can shut down all of our oil and gas supply, as we have already seen such a push to do so.

Another outlandish idea is that millions of people are being pushed to migrate due to Climate change, another Marxist tool used instead of calling it what it is: open borders!

All the hysteria over Climate change is handy.

Which is more probable: Is climate change caused by human industrial activity, or is it all part of a vast, well-planned hoax to brainwash people to believe the deception to gain control over the masses?

The apparent explanation is that understanding a Marxist concept is the root of climate change.

Researching Marxist ideology will make apparent to you the scheme that greedy, corrupt elitists and politicians use to usher in their utopian dreams.

It is sad, however, that many in society choose to be brainwashed because of a "fear tactic" projected upon them by evil individuals.

{ **13** }

THE OLIGARCH'S CONTROL

America has always faced a significant problem with established oligarchs.

The elites currently dismantle the Western regions, controlling media, the political establishment, and critical institutions. They have come a long way and broadened their influence on markets, banking, and trade to politics, social matters, and public health, and the influence is incomprehensive.

From the BLM riots, the January 6th disaster, the Russia gate scandal, the indictments of President Trump, all the imposition of several oppressive policies in the name of health were all influenced by the oligarchs, according to many sources.

The main concern should be the level of involvement this group has with other events to seek a more authoritarian government in the United States.

Cases in point are the government-imposed censorship, questions about presidential elections, destruction of food processing plants, train derailments, power grid attacks, the previous riots, the drag queen performances for young people, intense focus on gender matters, and high-profile public trials, simply random events during a time of significant social transformation, or are they actual indications among those who diligently observe the "signs" as instructed that God's patience, built on His immense compassion, is approaching its full extent.

The current era, known as the "church age," is rapidly coming to its conclusion, and the era that features God's severe Vengeance and His wrath is on the horizon.

We live in a society that is predominantly controlled by those who have effectively navigated down a path in which Satan has led them.

The path they choose to follow leads them to a depraved mindset that probably began long ago to many on behalf of their rebellion and rejection of the Highest.

It is fair to say that most of society's actions and behaviors witness a depraved mindset from just watching the evening news or entertainment.

The Progressive Cultural Change:

The Progressive's goal was to transform Western Culture in America using many methods, including teachings from the Frankfort School.

The Frankfort School's objective is to combine sociology, philosophy, psychology, and cultural theory to expand upon Marxist theory, known as Critical theory.

•One of their main objectives is to develop a critical theory of society that goes far beyond Marxism.

•Analyzing how culture and mass media influence and uphold social structure.

•The transformation within capitalist societies.

Many critical theorists who attended the Frankfort school looked to undermine and attack European cultural elements and how they could destroy them by using society.

As those theories became established and used in society, they began to attack every facet of their heritage that was left, such as religion, economics, government, the family, gender roles, ethical behavior, customs, sexuality, nationality, traditions, conservativism, loyalty, and patriotic pride.

Critical theorists acknowledged that conventional wisdom and the established social order needed to be dismantled and a "new thinking" that would eventually become an integrated part of the essential awareness.

Interestingly, celebrities, film, radio, music, and the latest television technology would promote the new thinking.

Lord Bertrand Russel's Work:

The Frankfort School and the Macy Group were involved with Bertrand Russel's work.

They were granted permission to radically alter American society through preexisting NGOs.

Bertrand Russel wrote in his book Impact of Science on Society in 1952. His book entailed progressive goals, using mass psychology as a way to brainwash the Culture. Its origin is built on occultism, and its critical tactics of using mass psychology are being carried out in the United States.

Its modern use is propaganda, which is most useful in education.

•They believe in capturing the minds of the young before they reach the age of 10.

•Using verses in music repeatedly.

•The influence of family is destructive.

•Christianity must be eradicated.

•To control their subjects accurately, every government must control education for over a generation and will not need police to control the masses.

It is progressive (communist) goals that originate in critical theory from the Frankfort School.

During the 1960s, the Beetles were used in music and television to change the Culture sweeping over England and the United States, capture the youth, and aid in the cultural revolution.

The Frankfort School aims to undermine the Christian beliefs in Western nations, including the United States, through sexual impulses, and they have achieved their goals successfully.

The public school system is fulfilling the progressive (communist) goals and continually bombarding youth using their mass psychological methods of gender theory, and the thousands of pronouns aid in the confusion of the youth, which is what they hoped for.

A List in Part of Their Goals:

•Create racial conflict continually.

•Using change as a method often causes uncertainty.

•Encouraging sexual orientation starts as young as age four.

•The breakdown of authority in schools and among teachers.

•Massive immigration destroys the identity of the Culture.

•The engagement of large consumptions of alcohol.

•Closing the churches.

•A flawed legal system with prejudices against victims and favor toward criminals.

•Reliance on government.

•Media manipulation and mental reduction.

•Promoting the disintegration of the family and parental authority.

Russel saw the transformation of cultural norms and traditions to produce depravity, destruction of the family, and the disposal of babies through abortions as a leftist goal for new thinking and, in his vision, a healthy society.

As we watch the transformation of a country by the Left here in America, it is crucial to understand the horrific outcome it is leading America on the pathway to a final one-world dictator, the Antichrist of (Revekation13), as the masses are already being conditioned to accept the engrossed blanket of evil that has descended upon a once free country but now entangled in a cultural transformation that has captured the minds of the young and old alike.

Another thought is that globalist billionaires harbor hatred against Christians and patriots, viewing them as a hindrance to their aim of establishing a borderless one-world government.

A new term has taken over the airways and social media: Christian Nationalist. Suddenly, such people who love the country, love God, and believe what the "founders" have always said, our rights given by God are now considered "bad" by the leftist mob.

The powerful elite does not think propaganda can sway patriots from their beliefs, which is why incarceration is the preferable method in silencing dissent, according to reports.

Ordinary people are no longer permitted to oppose leftists; if so, harsh punishments are implemented.

Elections have traditionally been the final determination of political legitimacy in the United States.

Credibility is supposed to be of utmost importance, but what appears out of all the ashes is "power." The individual who has you arrested is the one who holds all power.

A great example:

In a classic Orwellian move, the World Economic Forum's "Great Reset" aims to transform the globe into a destitute social detention camp where enslaved serfs "own nothing" and are thus happy and liberated.

It is just one example of the many methods of those who hold power and can transform a once "superpower" country into a reeducation camp for those who can't be swayed by such deception.

Investigating the WEF's Global Redesign Initiative might be a good idea. According to the Netherlands Transnational Institute, the "Initiative" suggests shifting focus from decision-making between government to a system of multi-stakeholder governance.

Put another way, they are subtly but surely replacing the established system of electing governments, who subsequently negotiate and ratify treaties, with one in which a self-selected group of "stakeholders" decides what is best for the world's populations.

It means that a globalist "economic" cartel, which is not elected, is driving humanity into serfdom, global poverty, and depopulation. Prominent transnational corporate "stakeholders" will decide where you live, what you eat (insects and weeds), how you reproduce (or not), how children produce carbon emissions (their belief), and what you can "rent" from them.

Now that they have acquired so much power, such powerful billionaire elitist can publicly declare their intentions to "move away from multilateral decision making" and replace it with a system of "multistakeholder governance."

A relatively straightforward proclamation of a new kind of supernational government is what the billionaires have planned. Only the wealthy oligarchs will hold control over humanity.

An oligarchy is a kind of government where only billionaire stakeholders have the authority to vote on whatever policies are put into effect.

But isn't it the "norm" already? In matters ranging from the environment, social and governance (ESG) concerns of vaccine passports, artificial intelligence (AI), a gain of function research, 15-minute cities, open borders, transhumanism, and even war, a small group of individuals, none of whom were elected to office are making all decisions on behalf of the populations of the world, reports have said.

How many of these unusual incidents in recent years do you think were orchestrated and executed by members of the deep state to aid a global agenda?

To "build back better, the slogan clearing the deck must be utilized to move away from intergovernmental decision-making and establish a multistakeholder governance framework.

It may shed light on the reason behind the brutal and on-going assault on our nation's heritage, customs, landmarks, religious beliefs, and founders.

According to sources, they aim to make us feel guilty, humiliated, and ashamed instead of idealists.

They aim to destroy not only history but also our shared principles, cultural legacy, dedication to individual liberties, and the entire concept of America.

They even try to shame you for your race and skin color.

Under the guise of opportunely random occurrences, the country is disintegrating; political divisions have widened on a much broader scale within just the past three to four years.

Public mayhem has risen as America's streets are invested with crime, and homelessness has reached an all-time high; the path is now open for a violent reorganization of power that our borders are flooded with gangs, terrorists, human trafficking, drug cartels, and so much more, according to reports.

Destroying the current governmental order is a prerequisite to establishing their "new order."

The Left of a country will continue to control what's left in a country.

{ 14 }

LAWLESSNESS

It seems that lawmakers from both parties would do everything they can to alleviate the nationwide crime wave and make America a safer place for everyone.

That is not what is being done. Even after an arrest, officials in our country are too lenient with violent offenders, releasing them back into society.

The situation is so bad that predators are everywhere, and it is only getting worse.

Bloomberg reports that violent deaths in Venezuela have significantly decreased due to substantial migration in recent years. It is excellent news for Venezuela.

Kristi Noem, a leading contender to be President Trump's possible running mate, has said, "They have been emptying their prisons of dangerous criminals to send them to America."

News out of Texas suggests that President Nicolas Maduro Moros, Venezuelan administrator, is secretly releasing prisoners, including those with violent convictions.

According to intelligence assessment, agents have seen the released inmates in migrant caravans that have been heading toward the U.S.–Mexico border.

An anonymous source told Breitbart Texas that the move is eerily similar to the boat left in the 1980s by Fidel Castro.

Elon Musk recently reacted to a report from X News that a Democrat from California is requesting more funds to provide beds in shelters that house migrants.

Musk mentioned in a post that the situation is so bad that dams are breaking nationwide. We Americans make up barely 4% of the global population. All necessary services would be overwhelmed if even one percent of the worldwide population relocates here. Musk went on to say, "The flood of illegals is crushing the country," and he was sounding the alarm.

Israel

Among many who have been vocal in recent weeks in pressuring Israel to recognize a two-state solution as a means of resolving the Palestinian-Israel conflict, Joe Biden has taken the lead in such a matter.

He insists on handing over the territory that is rightly Israel to the savage Hamas. It would also put Israel's enemies in a prime position to carry out their actual goal –the destruction of the Jewish state and the slaughter of its inhabitants.

The current administration and our nation's legislative entities show a clear desire for Israel to cease its military actions against Hamas and other terrorist groups.

The State Department provides instructions, objections,

and warnings to Israel urging agreement to stop the conflict. They appear to want to protect the terrorist commanders from punishment.

It is wrong for the administration to demand a two-state solution to satisfy the Palestinians. By doing so, Biden will acknowledge Hamas's brutality by granting them territory that legally belongs to Israel.

Furthermore, his suggestions would provide Israel's adversaries with a strategic advantage to achieve their ultimate goal, the destruction of the tiny state of Israel.

The United States exercised its veto power recently against a resolution demanding an immediate end to the fighting in Gaza.

Do not be deceived by the meaningless demonstration of solidarity with Israel. The Jewish people and Israel are not friends of the current administration.

The security of Israel and its people would be severely compromised if Bidens' suggestions were implemented.

The United States is in a precarious position as a result of the Biden administration's policies toward Israel for several reasons:

Our Nation Will Be Cursed Because of Incorrect Decision Toward Israel.

It would appear that the U.S. president and Secretary Blinken are dedicated to preventing Israel from crushing Hamas in its battle.

Despite their denials, Hamas would gain a strategic advantage and stronger negotiating position if it were to implement their suggestions, which would allow them to negotiate the release of hostages that they have not yet killed.

The caution from (Genesis 12:3) is relevant even now since Israel is a symbol of God's chosen people. (Romans 11:1-2). "I will bless those who bless you, and him who dishonors you I will curse, and in you, all the families of the earth shall be blessed."

What we will call a curse, or a judgment on those who would mock Israel like the Biden regime, is what the term "I will curse" means when it refers to God's reaction to those who treat His people, Israel, with contempt. It also refers to Christians. (2 Thessalonians 1:5-10).

The Biden administration's acts will undoubtedly bring a curse upon himself and those who support his policies, as well as the nation he represents, if the words of (Genesis 12:3) still apply to God's covenant with Abraham, which He reinforced to the descendants of Jacob in (Psalm 105: 7-11) and it does still apply.

God Will Surely Retaliate Against His Plan to Split The Land.

In the final days, God will punish people who try to partition His land, according to scripture.

The prophet Joel explains that the nation's ambition to partition "my land" is the root cause of God's wrath toward them at the end of the age. (Joel 3:1-3).

God will punish America for what Joe Biden and his administration have done in decisions toward Israel, as well as other essential methods implemented.

What we are witnessing concerning lawlessness and

corruption was predicted long ago in the ancient texts. All one must do is study biblical history to understand current events and their significance to bible prophecy. Unfortunately, that is no longer the case, as most of the population is no longer interested in anything the ancient texts have to say.

It, too, is a "prophecy" because we were forewarned that evil men and deceivers would worsen the closer, we got to the Lord's return.

Israel at war with Hamas will become worse, as all the Middle Eastern countries will be drawn into that war and surround Israel.

The dismantling of a country by the Leftists is also predicted in prophecy, as there will be a one-world government ruled by an evil tyrant known as the antichrist. The Lord allows the evil minions to speed up their process to allow the foretold prophecies to pass.

America is no longer the Christian nation it once was. God has removed His hand of blessing on a country that no longer recognizes Him, and Democrats have faced criticism on the topic of God and politics before. CBN initially reported in 2012 that God's name was excluded from the Democratic National Committee platform. The term "God-given" was also removed from the party platform in 2008.

As one who has thoroughly researched the ancient tests and has studied Bible prophecy and its significance to current events for over four decades, I stand in "awe" that God has not yet poured out His "wrath" on a degenerate and rebellious world.

The Biden administration's demands to divide the tiny nation of Israel is a serious concern, prophetically speaking.

We are watching in real-time; the world – stage is set concerning the "judgment" of God to soon fall on all those who have shaken their fits in God's face, daring Him to pass judgment. Still, horrors will commence upon all those who have "rejected" the Truth and chose to do things their way.

DEPOPULATION & MEDIA CONTROL

This year in the United States is an election year. During typical circumstances, an election represents the opportunity for regular individuals to regain authority over the future of their country. However, these are not ordinary circumstances.

Worldwide, individuals are becoming increasingly aware that governments have ceased to fulfill their duty to serve God and the people.

The globalist elites are determined to utilize the authority of national governments to execute a global reduction of humanity on Earth.

They aim to change the global population from approximately eight billion individuals to a mere one billion.

One can harbor doubts regarding the veracity of the claim. However, the fact that there is a limit of one billion is widely known.

Examine the recent remarks made by Dennis Meadows, who was involved in writing the 1972 manifesto for worldwide population reduction, known as "Limits of Growth" and reinforced by the Club of Rome.

"We are projected to reach a population of one billion people ... Getting back down is essential. That is what is to come."

The man who uttered the statement has precise knowledge of the future events that await humanity.

A group of wealthy globalists known as The Club of Rome has been working since 1968 to guarantee extinction, ensuring that many individuals, including ourselves, do not have prospects for the future.

Meadows has the following predictions for humanity:

•Food Shortages

•Pandemics

•Riots and Uprisings Globally

•Authoritarian Dictatorship

•A Decline in Living Standards

Hans Schellenberg, a climate scientist known for his radical views, was named to the Pontifical Academy of Science in 2014. He has recently agreed to reach a global population of one billion. He says the maximum number of people the planet can support "might be" less than one billion.

One of their methods is coercion and shame. Individuals will be pressured to have a reduced number of children. Furthermore, those considered unnecessary or surplus may be targeted.

Undoubtedly, the globalists have a clear intention to create harm.

In 2020, they disclosed their intentions on plans more openly and extensively than ever before:

•We were confined to our homes against our will.

•Our churches were shut down.

•They administered medical treatment that was proven harmful.

•They caused the breakdown in families.

•They caused worldwide job loss and contributed to a decline in our overall economic well-being.

Their objective is to achieve a global state characterized by reduced population, widespread poverty, and universal enslavement.

Anyone of good moral character would not like to witness any of the above outcomes.

However, globalists have long depended on mainstream media to subtly conceal the enormity and evilness of their plot from the public.

It is why the forces of evil consistently employ censorship of truthful information; it provides them with a small amount of additional time.

During the January 2024 meeting of the World Economic Forum in Davos, influential individuals' primary concern was devising strategies to prevent individuals from exchanging truthful information.

The European Commission (E.C.) president expressed to her colleagues at the World Economic Forum (WEF) that the primary issue of concern is the spread of disinformation and misinformation.

She was referring to the "truth," and the people who speak it are the ones they fear most.

During her remarks to those present at Davos, E.C. Vice President for Values and Transparency, Vera Jourova discussed:

The European Union is putting energy into ensuring the public has accurate information. We avoid discussing viewpoints. No one's views or vocabulary is being censored. I see that we are discussing the facts here.

It is directly taken from 1984 by George Orwell.

They will ensure we understand and acknowledge their "Factual Information."

The fundamental facts vital to us - the truths concerning God, life, and family – will be mercilessly repressed and dismissed as just subjective views.

They know we always come out on top when we speak the Truth.

The head of Internews, Jeanne Bourgault, addressed the World Economic Forum, mentioning,

We need to follow the money that disinformation makes. Spending a lot of money on substantial

Stuff is inevitable.

To direct their advertising budgets toward informative and encouraging content, you can put in a

lot of effort to compile lists of things to include and exclude "the news and information that is

accurate and relevant."

Please do not misunderstand; It pertains to the act of censoring honest media sources and reverts

back to the dominance of media outlets controlled by globalists.

George Soros Buys into Media

George Soros is a highly influential and potentially harmful individual in the

United States. The investor is determined to reshape the country according to his liberal

ideology, affecting not just our foreign policy agenda but the criminal justice system as well.

George Soros, a liberal billionaire, has ties to 54 high-profile members of the media, according

to a new study by the Media Research Center. Reporters, organizers, contributors, editorial staff,

broadcasters, and journalists are all part of the group reported by Dan Schneider and Joesph

Vazquez.

A person working for founded new network of Soro's was seen visiting the Biden White House

Over 20 times in less than a month. Fox News reported.

The upcoming election may be the most critical in our lifetime. Depending on who enters the

The Oval Office may determine whether this country can survive. The global forces of evil can

Make great strides forward if the outcomes are bad.

The globalist cabal wants to eliminate 7 billion people.

The truth-tellers must continue to enlighten those unaware of what is happening behind the scenes, as the dark storm clouds are increasing at an advanced pace as evil minions continue

on their quest toward an oppressive and demonic control of world government.

The Breakdown of Society

What is the underlying connection that links each of the following together?

•The suggestion is to consume insects and mealworms to preserve the Earth.

•Movies and other media outlets prioritize indoctrination over amusement and enjoyable entertainment purposes.

•Incompetent and psychologically unstable individuals who identify as transgender and occupy positions of power.

•The act of justice officials who choose not to imprison offenders.

•Our firms and institutions prioritize hiring employees based on diversity, equity, and inclusion (DEI) rather than hiring individuals by qualifications.

•It was stigmatizing "white males" in a manner that caused them to disengage from the Culture.

•Skyrocket inflation by engaging in unprecedented wasteful spending.

•Appointing a pair of the most influential individuals in a nation who possess such high levels of corruption and ineffectiveness that they cannot be relied upon to do the essential task of cleaning a restroom.

Each of the above is intended to undermine the overall morale of society.

What is the incentive for manipulating society?

Answer: To facilitate the influence and domination of individuals by the wealthy and powerful.

Who are the individuals or groups that have clearly expressed their desire to "Reset" the global economy and society without seeking our consent? The Internationalists, their supporters, and the misinformation they use in mainstream media and news outlets.

What is the reason behind their decision to undertake such radical action?

Answer: They have decided to take complete control of the world, similar to Hitler's onslaught, after realizing that people no longer have any moral courage, and they are advancing at an alarming rate.

Psychological operations aim to demonstrate to one's adversary that any form of opposition is pointless and to induce defeat in individuals due to the perception of a powerful adversary.

It is not science fiction that is employed; instead, psychological procedures are actual and are being implemented today.

Furthermore, it is not beings from outer space that run them. A global conspiracy is carrying out atrocities.

The goal of the authoritarian elites is not scientific and technological advancement but worldwide dominance.

A Satanic Utopia is their goal, and they intend to achieve it by enslaving humanity.

They plan to lower and break the spirit of the resistance to accomplish their agenda.

They want all resisters and anyone who challenges their agenda to join their cause or flee.

In a nation governed by religions and principles, dictators must employ "rebel" strategies to undermine their adversaries' sense of purpose.

To establish influence over the majority, a select few will employ rapid and frequent assaults to assess the determination of their adversary.

When the opponent becomes downtrodden and ceases to resist, proceeding with more aggressive measures becomes feasible.

The malevolent leftist elites have grown shameless to the point where they openly express their desire to dominate and oppress the public, and the ability to accomplish it did not occur suddenly.

A series of carefully executed actions gradually eroded the determination of our country and the rest of the globe.

The despicable leftist bureaucrats recruited magistrates during the twentieth century and had them declare school prayer and bible reading to be invalid.

After realizing the country lacked the "faith" to resist, they proceeded to even more widespread anarchy. They created new rights, such as "the right to privacy," and these magistrates were able to legitimize abortion on a national level.

Many now realize the vile leftist goal in implementing such a "ruling" was to further their depopulation objective. In terms of valid law, the decision was utterly irrelevant.

The globalist took their victory as a green light to forward their radical agenda, asserting that the Constitution of the United States has always protected sexual orientation, legalizing "gay marriage," and recognizing the existence of non-binary sex.

They made excellent use of the fact that the faith of many American believers was considerably shattered.

The time finally came that as many Americans were cut off from God's message book, the Bible, they would be more inclined to accept any manifestation of godlessness and corruption.

Currently, instead of engaging in bible reading and Prayer in schools, children are now being exposed to gay pornography and literature that pedophiles approve of, and some, not all, parents and grandparents are delighted that their children are being taught queer theory, as God is now kicked out of the equation.

Morally strong individuals have started to disappear from the faith, and as a result, evil is spreading around the globe, and fewer individuals are taking a stand to stop it.

Believers are currently marginalized in a country that has a constitution that safeguards our rights. However, the Constitution does not recognize that it protected its citizens less than a decade ago.

Given Satan's involvement in the demoralization industry, it is expected that his followers are also engaged in the same type of work. They are clearly recognized as actively opposing anything good, decent, and upright in God's divine order.

Example: God said, 'Be fruitful and multiply." It is not

unusual that individuals who serve Satan would seek to resist God's instructions.

The devil has identified those individuals, including those who perform abortions, who actively challenge and prevent the implementation of that directive.

That evil entity had to form a cult to oppose God's instruction to "subdue the Earth" when God uttered His plan.

To persuade individuals to adopt a pagan mindset centered around living in harmony with nature, Satan would require a fabricated storyline.

Therefore, the concept of "climate change" was conceived, and the devil must exert relentless efforts to ensure he maintains domination over his realm.

He requires influential individuals to ensure that everyone remains aligned with his objectives.

Their primary responsibility is to establish the right situation that will enable an alternation in the divine order God established.

Presently, he is choosing malicious left-wing elites to deliberately cause chaos in various societies of the world and dismantle them, as we have seen demonstrated in the United States within the past few years.

Due to their limited numbers and inability to conquer the world through force, good and decent people cannot be easily bought, as most will have to be disheartened until they surrender to the power of wealthy, depraved globalizers.

Satan is mindful of the fact that, as human beings, we are not capable of effectively serving both God and money since our affection would be directed toward one and despise the other.

Locating those who favor wealth over devotion to God is not challenging.

Observe the present state of the medical profession or science right now.

It does not take long for corrupt politicians and professionals to seize power and rearrange God's creation to benefit themselves. Satan has rewarded them the world for their submissions to his authority.

Just as the devil tempted Jesus on the mountaintop and showed him all the kingdoms of the world he would give Jesus if He would bow down just one time and worship him (Jesus rebuked him), the devil has offered such wealth to the globalizers and those that submit to them, as they have changed the divine order to a depraved mindset in individuals who call evil good and good evil; who groom young children confusing them that there are more than two genders; dismantling the police to keep law and order, instead choose crime and lawlessness to run rampant in towns and cities and burning down businesses and looting as they riot in the streets.

Flying illegals into the country, not vetting them, and releasing terrorists and violent criminals in the streets of America; involvement with a country's enemies in exchange for millions of dollars, greed, and power.

The globalizer's initial objective is to remove those they consider "rebels" who threaten their objective, and their focus is the Christians, as they are the most significant challenge to Satan's empire.

Malignant elitists utilize their riches and influence to erode the morale of their adversary, and tricking a large group of people requires significant financial resources and influence.

Regarding the goal of the nefarious Leftists to exert control over the entire planet, an immeasurable quantity of wealth will be rewarded to achieve their plans.

Western Civilization has posed its most significant challenge in this present era. It is why Western Civilization is consistently criticized in our educational institutions, which serve as venues for indoctrination and propaganda spreading.

Evil minions use an all-out effort to debase white males, and the unjustified allegation of "racism" is becoming more widespread among the wicked; it is deeply rooted in our society and is employed by cunning individuals to provide false testimony against white males.

Among the wicked globalizers, white males are the main target of demoralization; despite the accusations of "racism," white men have always been the most vocal advocates for equality and freedom and the strongest advocates for spreading the gospel.

Examining the Declaration of Independence, the Constitution, the Civil War, the movement for the abolition of slavery, World War 11, and various other historical events, it is evident that "white men" have consistently played a prominent role in advocating for freedom.

The deliberate actions of the wealthy left-wing bureaucrats, who predominantly consist of "white males," indicate their intentions to control and suppress this particular ethnic group.

They have sought the backing of hostile Caucasian communist at the community level to advance their plans.

They attempt to secure the assistance of other minority groups, but their level of achievement has fallen short of their expectations.

The influence of artificially created organizations such as BLM is fading; it appears that when malicious individuals of Caucasian descent inspire other ethnicities to harbor hatred towards morally upright individuals of Caucasian descent, they become entangled in the resulting conflict.

In the present moment, if one were to express a discriminatory attitude based on race, it would be appropriate to direct societal outrage at the malevolent globalizers, specifically the malicious "white communist."

All those individuals are considered inferior to the rest of humanity due to their evolutionary lineage from monkeys. Suppose you are skeptical of it, simply research. It is not a secret!

Among all ideologies aimed against humanity, the bogus science of evolution is most disheartening.

Those hell-bent on destroying humanity would do anything to make people believe that their lives don't matter, and that spiritual degeneration is what it is.

The core tenet of evolution is that all things come into

existence through unforeseen events, not because God created them.

God brought into existence the celestial realm and the planets, and Satan required a way by which he might dispute that claim, and a morally corrupt population has widely embraced his response.

Most humans mistakenly believe that their existence is nothing more than a simple occurrence. To accept such a claim, the search for Goodness, Affection, and Truth is unworthy of consideration. As a result, all principles of virtuous behavior can be effortlessly eradicated.

Satan knows he must drive a wedge between people and God's scripture, which is His Holy Bible, and when he triumphs, we become defenseless against an entity that is many times more intelligent than us. His henchmen will then Rule over many.

When a society forsakes God's divine Word, altering the established order that God created becomes more convenient.

It is particularly evident in the realm of sexuality. God declared that He created two distinct genders, male and female; a significant portion of the population is successfully persuaded by Satan and his followers that genders are reversible.

By elevating their people to authority, the rich and powerful have made sure that evildoers face no penalties; on the other hand, they make sure that anyone who opposes them will soon find themselves out of work, subject to ridicule, high court settlements, and many times behind bars.

Most people will give up and surrender to the new evil after a few high-profile assaults on "the opponents who are trying to keep their dignity.

When a society rebels against God, it is more likely to be subdued by evil.

Indeed, the vile global-minded are running the show in the entertainment business, and their goal in releasing the rot is to quench the spirit and dishearten any males left with any appearance of manhood.

The malevolent leftist elites exert significant influence over the entertainment industry and show no opposition to its potential demise.

They aim to undermine the morale of society; hence, they will insist that the entertainment business circulates low-quality content or cease to exist.

The corrupt elite doesn't care about quality entertainment, and many have noticed that many businesses no longer care about the people they serve or investors.

They have a new interest: to change society according to the demands of the liberal leftists.

One of the company's new priorities is peddling "social justice."

For example, Budweiser hired an unsavory person to represent its beer, and Target offended the public by selling alluring products during the holiday season.

Such businesses no longer have good service; their only objective is to prevent the people from being defiant to the mission that the globalizers are accomplishing.

Such nefarious individuals have successfully bought or

bribed the majority of corrupt politicians or removed any who oppose their plan; by doing so, they can employ a range of toxic ideologies, such as DEI, CRT, and various other damaging concepts, to dismantle societal structures.

It appears the progressives prefer humanity to consider killers and rapists as sufferers of the community and condemn conservative people; such people are deemed inadequate by the Left, and it is why they need to shut them up, bankrupt, be jailed, or be removed from society.

The wealthy global-minded officials understand that letting those who commit crimes run wild in the culture makes everyone afraid and less motivated, which makes it easier to oppress and be able to rule an authoritarian government.

The demonic realm works through the physical in influential individuals by calling men "toxic masculine" or "mansplaining" to make them feel weak so that no one stands up to the liberal bureaucrats.

The goal is not to have any males resist their perverse agenda, and it is another lesson why they hate "alpha males" and want to remove all masculinity from the planet.

It is how Satan is actively working through ignorant people by breaking down society, thus, the divine plan of God.

Currently, in this civilization, God's anger is being shown against the perverse and lawless people who hide from the truth.

The devil and his depraved utopia builders, the white communists, and anyone else who joins in their insanity know that God has made His word clear to them; everything created makes it possible for humanity to see and understand God's majestic handprint and His eternal power and divine nature; therefore, they are without excuse.

Powerful rulers dominate significant journalistic sources and the global media infrastructure, and their authority is solely derived from the power society grants them.

They have intentionally twisted God's divine order, but that doesn't mean we must cave into their depraved insanity.

The individuals claiming that "truth-tellers" are spreading disinformation or misinformation need to be held accountable.

They deserve zero creditability when they utilize "fact auditors" to manipulate the truth.

Furthermore, it is the responsibility of children's parents and grandparents to prevent such people from corrupting the upcoming generation with their anti-God ideologies and perversions.

If you are depressed because of the blanket of rot surrounding you in the cultural decline, it is appropriate to attribute the situation to authoritarian bureaucrats.

As mentioned, all of the incidents are a deliberate effort to undermine the morale of upright and respectable individuals in this nation and around the globe. Their actions are to demoralize anyone who is left who still believes in the divine order and to weaken our will so that we give in and join their debased plan or battle the legal system in court appearances.

All we can do at this time is alert those who will listen that an engineered plan is being carried out by perverse and depraved individuals who are working to establish a godless one-world government and have zero tolerance for any individual who still believes in the divine order and resists the rot that they are using to demoralize humanity.

When decent and respectable people are confronted with severe demoralization tactics, it is essential not to cave into the wicked plots of the unregenerate.

Those of us who hold to the faith will likely be defeated in every dispute over culture. Still, it is imperative to remember that Jesus warned us about the breakdown in societies around the globe and the difficult times we, as believers, would face in this last-day generation.

We are currently experiencing an unprecedented breakdown in society by a demoralizing operation instituted by an anti-nationalist hierarchy that believes they have transcended to god status and are the caretakers of the Earth.

Never before in the history of a country have we seen an onslaught of such radical policies introduced to the public that is determined to invade the soul, mind, and body of each individual on Earth.

Their determination and motivation come solely from the demonic realm they have given themselves to be ruled and dominated by. They will continue building their new Tower of Babel until the Highest stands up and says, "Enough."

According to the prophetic teachings in the ancient texts, that day is soon to be upon us, and those who have shaken their fits in God's face by twisting the divine order and individuals who have joined them will face God's wrath when it is poured out upon everyone left behind on Earth.

Humanity is currently facing divine punishment from God, and the imminent arrival of Jesus Christ to call His faithful Home to be with Him is now at the door.

Don't be left behind to face the horrors to come. Jesus is our only Hope in a darkened world. He is the "light" in that darkness!

DESPITEFUL OF TRUTH

Civilization cannot persist in a culture that rejects truth, as that society will reject reality.

Those in power on the left in the country seem to have such an attitude.

The focus is that reality is not something you can pick and choose from; we live in a world of reality contrary to the desires of specific individuals running the WHO, WEF, UN, and other world leaders.

Consider those who are not happy with God and His plan for humanity.

Truth must be taken seriously; otherwise, an individual will deceive himself.

Some will say truth is defined by how an individual perceives it.

I am referring to God's truth, as there is none other, regardless of how one wants to interrupt it.

Of all the interpretations individuals want to use, God's truth is the highest sphere that cannot be reckoned with.

However, many have altered the truth to fit the narrative when needed.

Consider N.Y. city is going bankrupt because of the 64,800 illegal immigrants, costing the city $387 a day for each immigrant they shelter and provide food to.

At that price, N.Y. city pays $9.15 billion a year.

Under the Biden administration, the "executive organizations" are responsible for N.Y. city falling apart because government programs and associations for culture will be cut completely.

The "reality" and "truth" cannot be denied in such a dire situation.

Unless the country is entrenched under challenging circumstances, such as an attack from outside sources on our infrastructure or full-scale war, the sole event that could capture the general population's interest is an economic meltdown.

Most people are not concerned by the "truth" of the reality of many harmful events in our country and world.

Examples of Distortion of Truth:

•Consider the truthfulness and motivations of party leadership, which should be on your radar if you vote for a particular party.

For most of its history, the Democratic Party has silenced and disqualified votes, even as it accused its opponents of engaging in similar things.

Some party leadership will consistently tell you that their opponents are attempting to marginalize votes to destroy democracy. Still, the truth is that the assertion backs up their lies in the public square.

In a recent statement, Attorney General Merrick Garland referenced the post-civil War history of voter fraud, suggesting that other groups used aggression to limit Black Americans' right to vote.

Still, he asserts today that measures to verify the identity of votes attempt to limit and diminish voting rights.

For some reason, Garland seems oblivious that the Constitution specifies who can vote in elections.

Leading officials deny those who can vote the chance to cast a ballot by preventing any verification about voting eligibility.

Even while Garland would like to bring up the Civil War and Jim Crow, they were a deliberate attempt by a Party to deny Black Americans the right to vote.

These laws enforced segregation in public schools, public spaces, public transit, housing, restrooms, water fountains, and restaurants for almost a century.

The dismantling of the laws started with the 1965s Voting Rights Act and the 1964s Civil Rights Act.

However, the left at various levels of government vehemently fought those reforms, persisting in their opposition until the 1970s.

Globalizers advocate that each vote should be considered valid and noteworthy while asserting that their rivals are undermining the basis of democratic governance.

Consider the diligent efforts to eliminate Donald Trump from the ballot.

He has been penalized, his enterprises have been banned, and laws have been manipulated to convict him.

To tap it all off, they had their state officials unlawfully remove him from the ballot and every step taken to safeguard democracy.

However, their message is that you must vote for the nominee they select.

It is an act of severe denial of the right to vote!

Moreover, it is not solely Trump whom they are targeting.

Anyone who deviates from the established norms is the primary focus of attention.

•Law Abiding Citizens Classified as Criminals While the True Offenders are Protected:

How stupid do they think we are?

It is widely known at this time that the regime and its enforcement agencies want all guns confiscated so that the average citizen no longer protects themselves and that only common criminals can own guns.

These actions are pursued with the illusion of safeguarding us, yet they are forms of disinformation and deceit.

At the expense of the working class, the criminals prefer to remain united and defend each other; unfortunately, they are the ones in control.

As mentioned, recall the instances of theft, arson, property destruction, and violent assaults that occurred during the deceitful plan known as "COVID," primarily carried out by the communist organization of BLM and Antifa.

The authorities and security forces intentionally permitted its situation, as minimal arrests and convictions existed.

Reflect for a moment on how the authorities and its associates fully supported the riots and violent looting of retail stores, malls, and other businesses and how it continues to this day.

Authorities even went as far as to say that stealing goods valued at close to $1,000 without any concern of punishment was safe.

It served as a deliberate incentive for attackers to engage in theft.

Many people were either tackled or jailed for trying to stop these criminals from looting and damaging properties.

Consider that the country and its security agencies are diligently gathering individuals from all over the world and allowing them to cross the border and enter the country, then offering them abundant benefits, including free housing, medical care, education, and transportation to any destination they desire.

By doing this, the regime has managed to deceive the naïve and reliant citizens of the nation into placing the responsibility on those entering the U.S. through permission and even blaming President Trump rather than on its officials and illicit accomplices who are responsible for engineering and orchestrating its fraudulent scam.

The globalizers win despite what is right and wrong.

They strongly desire to establish the country's "Reset" into their one-world utopian government.

They will not stop until the plan is complete.

The country's leader has said he plans to finish the job, and the globalizers will see that it gets done.

They may drag him across the finish line until they complete the job they have set out to do, not caring about you, the American citizen, the Constitution, or any other distraction standing in their way.

It is why there is so much corruption in government and why they incite unpunished criminal activity, civil disorder, and chaos, and a significant portion of the foolish population willingly complies with their objective, no questions asked.

A problematic situation such as the one we are experiencing could potentially result in the confinement of individuals within the U.S. behind physical barriers to prevent movement. In contrast, the uniformed working class is deceived into believing such measures are aimed at preventing the entry of others.

The grand plan is to allow the economy to collapse and wipe out the system that allows food production and distribution possible – making life extremely difficult for everyone – destroy the present monetary system and replace it with a digital I.D. and digital currency for everyone – all to seize control of the entire population.

Enormous discontentment is required to carry out such an intentional and organized scheme of devastation and restart the economy, which will rob individuals of everything they own, their quality of life, leaving people in a dreadful state of unhappiness and depression, leading them to be more reliant on government.

Serfdom is what awaits the average individual as they now blatantly announce their plans openly.

Complete military control or martial law is possible in

the not-to-distant future because of what we have witnessed thus far, what the globalizers are announcing on their websites, and the corruption and criminality continuing.

Whatever the case, an alternative police state is on the horizon.

Unless the culture can come to terms with the "truth" unfolding even now, it will be more susceptible to blaming others rather than putting the blame where it belongs—on a corrupt cabal of influential individuals—your real opponents. It will be more controlled by the masters it willingly entrusted with for the rest of their lives, not to mention the younger generation and what they will experience.

The right to self-defense does not require the consent or authorization of any unlawful or unethical authority since it is a fundamental human right.

To be safe and free, citizens must protect themselves at all costs.

A peaceful and healthy culture relies on nonviolence. However, when the authorities turn hostile and declare war on their people, it becomes an entirely different situation.

It then becomes necessary to defend oneself and their family at all costs against the oppressor.

•Think back to the 2020 elections and how they funded Fusion GPS to manufacture a narrative that Trump was collaborating with Russia.

The report was essential in Obama obtaining a FISA secret court warrant to conduct surveillance on President Trump's campaign.

The appointment of a special prosecutor following the

election resulted in an investment of millions of dollars by the wealthy bureaucrats to establish President Trump's negligence. They produced nothing.

What are the implications of surveillance on topics like Covid, the border, out-of-control inflation, Hunter Biden, China, January 6th, shutting down of family farms in Oregon, food processing plants burning down, the supply chain, election fraud, censoring free speech, reducing our energy supply, Congress, the Supreme Court, and Constitution being overridden by a select group? No one is held accountable!

In this setting, the corrupt bureaucrats have taken advantage of funds from taxpayers to develop computerized intelligence technologies to direct our information.

Corrupt individuals have used political and financial influence to force large corporations, news outlets, internet companies, and other entities to circulate propaganda.

It appears we are currently living under an escalating authoritarian system, which is backed by an opposition group but also by the entire state infrastructure we live under.

A war is being waged on the country with the infiltration of thousands of illegals entering the southern border daily, and reports have come out that staging areas across the nation of young males of immigration status who are either of military or syndicated mob, housed in facilities similar to dorms.

This scene undoubtedly shows an army or terrorist holding location, as everyone involved in a conflict region is familiar with it.

Furthermore, the authorities are cracking down on the few remaining opponents in America and worldwide.

•Why were most generals and other military personnel purged from the military or forced to retire who still believed in defending the country and protecting American citizens?

Why did West Point recently remove Duty, Honor, and Country from its military creed?

Why did Biden cancel the funding for building our new aircraft carriers while Russia and China expanded theirs?

Thoughts To Consider:

•They have WOKE the Military.

•They have Transgendered the Military.

•They have purged the Military.

Why? It does not take much to connect the dots!

Sources have reported that recruiters have difficulty finding people to enlist, and males are not reenlisting after serving their term, while more women stay in the military.

Is it possible that they will put women on the front lines in the event of war? God forbid if that be the case. It is in the genetic makeup that women are more emotional than men. Think about the consequences if that is the case.

IDOLATRY & JUDGMENT

Church history has revealed national sins that could cause God to turn His back on a country.

The ancient text has disclosed national transgressions that have led to the divine abandonment of a nation.

•Unappreciative: Being ungrateful is an act of national transgression.

The biblical text in The Book of Judges recounts the repetitive cycle of revolt, vengeance, forgiveness, and recovery that occurred in Israel a total of 13 times.

The prophet Jeremiah told them to remember all the blessings bestowed upon them. He continued to warn them that if they remained unappreciative and ignorant, it would provoke God's judgment, and it happened.

It would be wise for America to heed Jeremiah's advice, but we have moved far past such a warning.

•Idolatry: The act of idolatry, which refers to false gods and idol worship, is considered a grave offense to God against a country.

Keep in mind anything that becomes more important to us than God can be considered an idol.

It is best to ponder our hearts for a moment and consider our personal relationship with Him.

In our modern era, idol worship does not mean bowing down to a statue or golden calve to worship it; it can take a softer method.

A Few Examples of Idol Worship:

Identity: When we put our love for God behind our self-image, accomplishments, and social standing, we idolize ourselves.

Frequently, we look to these parts of our identity for reassurance and meaning:

Occupation: achieving professional goals and being well respected in one's field can be time-consuming.

An idol is created when labor takes precedence over a person's worship of God.

Wealth-belonging and Financial Stability can easily override our spiritual health in our quest for material wealth and prosperity and our desire to fit in with a specific group.

The ideology of materialism can gradually divert us from our spiritual connection to God.

Entertainment & Media: We risk losing sight of God in our adoration of worldly pleasures like movies, sports, social media, music, and Hollywood stars.

When these things consume our lives, they become idols.

Physical Image: It can become an idol if one is overly concerned with meeting beauty standards, having an upbeat view of their body image, and being physically appealing.

Our outward appearance might take precedence over our true nature.

Ease & Convenience: Being in a comfortable position throughout life can slowly undermine our dependence on God.

An idol is created when material comfort prioritizes personal and spiritual development.

Technology & Electronic Devices: Cell phones, video games, and other social media have the potential to separate us from our connection to God.

Home & Family: Home and family are a source of joy, but they can become objects of excessive devotion if we place them above our love and connection to God. Prioritizing the achievements and wellness of our children can also take priority over our connection to God.

Is it Too Late For America?

(Isaiah 6) "It's too late. You would not listen, you wouldn't see, you will not believe, and now you can't."

"Tell them it is too late. Judgment is already in motion."

The verse is a warning and should be taken seriously.

How do we know when it is too late?

The answer to that question is found in (Romans 1).

It is when a country is steeped in profound perversion. When godless leaders send out letters to high-ranking officials telling them there is nothing wrong with cross-dressing in their ranks and somehow prioritize in an attitude like a daily briefing on the subject matter and comparable behavior patterns, all the while, when much more serious attention should be given to governing a country that needs such dire repair.

A blood bath for full-term babies to be aborted encourages it.

The lunacy of a warped mindset is when individuals legislate great evil and criminalize morally and upright people.

It is then when a country is under God's judgment.

It is crucial to read (Romans 1).

It is, then, when a country is under God's judgment.

When society has reached that point (corporately speaking) in a country, it is nationally under God's judgment phase.

When judgment falls on society, God Himself finally warns individuals to "repent" of their sins before His Wrath is poured out.

In other words, judgment always falls before His wrath, and then it is too late.

Why do I say this?

Researching early biblical texts is a proven and accurate message to all of us about what to expect when a society has reached its rebellion stage against God. Further punishment to the people is when their leaders intentionally reverse the laws of God and natures God.

When this happens, individuals are turned to a "reprobate mindset."

(Romans 1) He warns that God will send a delusional spirit to those who reject the truth and believe a lie.

There is nothing a person can do then; at that point, their mind is already warped because God turned them over to delusional thinking because they refused the "truth" when He was striving to get their attention, and they said No.

If you are asking yourself the question, what happened to the country, (Romans 1) gives you the answer.

However, there is a small minority of people who are exempt from judgment; Christians have nothing to fear. They said Yes to Jesus.

{ **18** }

DIVERSITY

At one time in the history of the traditional United States, it mandated that immigrants assimilate and adopt American culture, but this is no longer the case.

The United States today embraces variety today, which entails a flood of immigrants from all over the world, each with their unique language, culture, and set of beliefs and principles.

In case you have not noticed, the country you once were familiar with is no longer your country, and your children and grandchildren no longer live in same America you grew up in; if they are of white ethnicity, you can expect them to experience many struggles and hardships.

Diversity is a "tool" used to water down a culture and embrace a culture of immigrant- invaders.

The Western world is undergoing significant damage due to the implementation of multiculturism.

Massive numbers of immigrant invaders are eradicating

the ethnic existence of every white ethnicity, including British, Swedish, Dutch, French, German, and Italian.

The Tower of Babel & Multiculturism

Some on both sides of the political spectrum are erecting a new Tower of Babel, so they must have multiculturism to proceed with their agenda of "Resetting" the country.

Nations are composed of a uniform population, yet in America, society does not have a common language, belief, or culture.

Diversity politics drives a wedge between citizens, making it impossible for them to unite against government tyranny.

Just as the European Union aims to eradicate nationalism in Europe to remove identities, such as Dutch, Italian, and German, as they integrate into Europe, their individual culture fades from historical memory.

Let us not forget the tearing down of historical statues throughout the country, as well as no longer teaching American history in the schools and changing other curricula, such as math, calling it racist, and other insane motives.

All the crazy and bizarre actions that took place in the country and continue being used to transform the country and to accommodate the arrival of millions of immigrants; therefore, destroy the statues, make education simple so that your children will not have to be challenged, and all students will be on the same learning level, keeping in mind one thing though, only the upper-class hierarchy's children will have quality education, not your children, because "serfs" are the lower class in the new utopia they are building.

Their plan for civilization is only two classes of people—the privileged elites and serfs.

Few, if any, Americans understand the gravity of the threat they and their children and grandchildren will face.

The liberal regime in power, under their set of laws, already considers Americans second-class citizens.

White students are indoctrinated in educational institutions to despise their parents and blame themselves and their parents for the enslavement and tyranny of "people of color."

They are also educated on the possibility that their biological gender does not accurately represent who they are.

How much more insanity will be displayed by their warped mindset?

Where are the parents? Where are the dads? Do they even care about the dire possibilities their offspring are subjected to?

The white society is undergoing significant damage to its social structure, physical well-being, and mindset.

It is vital to understand that anti-God U.N. officials backed a plan that was published in a document twenty years ago titled "Replacement Migration."

The tearing down of America and the "Reset" of the country is all by design.

We started hearing the term multiculturism during the Obama tenure.

Obama is concerned with the worldview he has internalized, which is influenced by a heavily influenced learning ideology of diversity that does not prioritize American exceptionalism.

Obama's perspective is a product of a lifelong friendship with anti-American figures, including Rev. Jeremiah Wright, Bill Ayers (head of the Weather Underground and bomber at the Pentagon), and Bernardine Dohrn, who was Ayers's fugitive wife.

It is a school of thought by professors of how the Islamic barbarism of today is morally equivalent to what the Catholics did centuries ago during the Inquisition.

It is what students of today are being taught in universities on Diversity and multiculturism.

The students embrace and advocate for the honoring and reverence of all societies, traditions, and civilizations.

They believe that Western standards of conduct that are "higher" than those of other nations are an example of racist European Imperialism.

Why not question a campus multiculturalist who supports the concept of radical similarity: Is the practice of enforced mutilation of female genitalia that is practiced in over thirty different countries in sub-Saharan Africa, as well as the Middle East, ethically comparable to other values associated with traditional beliefs? Is the custom of enslavement in Sudan and Nigeria considered an ethnic comparable?

Driving, voting, and attending school are just a few of the many restrictions imposed on women in the Middle East.

Some cultures, under Islamic law, call for the death penalty of stoning for females who commit adultery, and they also cut off the fingers of those who are thieves.

Specific individuals who advocate for cultural diversity

are affiliated with university organizations that support the lesbian, gay, bisexual, and transgender community.

They need to inquire about the level of acceptance the Muslim society would have for their way of life.

If I'm not mistaken, they consider it a crime and throw gays off the rooftops and other harsh methods that lead to death.

Essential to the concept of Diversity is a direct assault on Christianity.

There have been efforts by local school boards to prohibit Christmas music that features Jesus Christ or symbols of faith associated with Christmas.

Because they contained references to God and Christianity, historical materials transcribed by one instructor were forbidden from being used in the classroom by one school district. Samuel Adam's "Rights to the Colonists" and the Declaration of Independence were part of the dispute.

The stability of Western principles is in danger on university campuses around the United States; they are being brutally assaulted by the educational establishment.

Their goal includes limiting individuals' freedoms in favor of more government regulations, elevating entitlements over equality, and stopping technological progress in the name of nature worship.

Communists and other leftists oppose free market Capitalism and Christianity because Christian countries have always enjoyed financial freedom and have always stood for individual liberty and property rights.

The U.N. has always fought to remove property rights and instead distribute wealth.

The "Replacement Migration" policy they adopted twenty years ago is coming to pass.

It is why Klaus Schwab, head of the WEF, said, "You will own nothing and be happy."

Sadly, the public is not concerned, and the globalizers are aware of it.

They understand that when the public is dumbed down, how easy it will be to overcome and control them; it is just a little trick communists use and can be found in their "communist manifesto."

For those who seek domination over the lives of others, individual freedoms, and property rights are inherently evil, they believe, and it is a big part of their plan to take over Western culture.

Pay attention to the invasion at the border and the millions of immigrants that have entered.

However, there are Constitutional laws that are being ignored; not only are the borders wide open to all, terrorists, enemies of the country, and more, but what tops the absurdity is that recently, news reports stated that the chartering of flights from other countries and flying all different cultures of people directly into the United States, anywhere they want to go, and guess who is paying for it? Your taxes.

Can it get any more insane than it is now?

I cannot give you false hope; the future looks grim, and even though it appears that all races and ethnicities that live here are being cared for, it is only temporary; anyone who is not part of the hierarchy mob, in their resetting of the country and world, is considered the lower class, and those that make it through what is coming, will serve their affluent masters.

THE ROMAN EMPIRE, WASHINGTON DC AND JESUS

If revealing an unlawful behavior is considered illegal, then society is in a dire situation.

In other words, speaking the truth nowadays about injustice in the political arena can have you watched and censored and worse.

Amidst the present political environment, holding to one's moral convictions and being courageous in speaking the truth about oppressive regimes might swiftly label you a threat to the state.

Remaining quiet in the presence of corruption and depravity is an easy endeavor.

What is more complex is the absence of individuals with moral fortitude willing to stand for our liberties and denounce the multiple types of evil perpetuated by a regime.

The corrupt Roman Empire of Jesus Day is comparable to the Western Empire of the United States today.

The Elite Rule:

With increased division between the rich and poor, the royalty and powerful merged, and the lower class was slowly stripped of their freedom of speech and assembly.

Mysteries surrounding the Roman Empire's internal affairs were just as prevalent as the contemporary United States due to the absence of the Empire's accountability, national spying, and affluent authority.

The wealthy rulers were on guard against any appearance of alleged risk to their control.

The Roman Empire used its army to police the people, enforce the peace, and ensure that all the rules were kept, including guarding prisons and executions.

In the United States, the FBI, Department of Justice, law enforcement, and Homeland Security are becoming more militarized.

In due time, Rome instituted a lasting military monarchy that subjected unrealistic and harsh tyrannical government.

The Western Empires of the world, including the United States, continually used surveillance on their citizens by tracking and censoring them as suspects, as the Roman Empire used the same harsh manner on its people.

Tracking, Censoring, Jesus:

During Jesus's earthly ministry, the Roman Empire labeled Him a revolutionary.

He was considered a threat to the supremacy of the

Roman Empire and to the religious leaders and high priests of that day.

They labeled Him a "radical" because He spoke the "truth" about the injustice done to the people of that day, and they charged Him with threatening the country's security.

How often in this country do we hear some bureaucrats and "propaganda broadcasters" proclaim that individuals standing for liberty and justice threaten Democracy?

It is used consistently by many in that group.

The similarities between the Western Empire in this era and the Roman Empire are comparable.

When Jesus was arrested and charged before Pontius Pilate, they said He was disrupting the political climate of that era. He spoke openly about the people being oppressed with high taxes and claimed to be a King.

The era of that day was a mandatory death sentence for any of those claims made, and they executed Jesus for it.

They wanted to make Him an example to anyone who dared to challenge the corruption in government at that time.

Jesus was arrested and charged with insurrection and leading the people in rebellion against the government.

His crucifixion was an immensely public statement of being convicted of "high treason." When He overturned the money changers in the temple, they considered it a crime of civil disobedience because the Jewish temple was considered the administrative headquarters of the Sanhedrin.

They arrested Jesus at night, and it was considered illegal

to do so, but the authorities overlooked the "rules" of that day and did it anyway.

Let us not forget the grimly striking resemblance to modern-day SWAT team operations under cover of darkness by a vast army of heavily armed troopers.

The Western Empire of our era has followed the Roman model of totalitarianism in its treatment of societal disagreement.

Jesus was charged as a political inciter of trouble, a revolutionary who challenged the status quo.

He stood against the political and religious system of that era.

He confronted their assertions of authority, and He fearlessly voiced the truth to those in authority at a time when such actions resulted in a harsh death penalty.

Regrettably, the revolutionary Jesus, the one who opposed the Roman Empire's harsh injustice and persecution, is disregarded nowadays.

Many church leaders today instruct their congregations to ignore the blatant depravity and injustice done in society, submitting to rulers who are blatantly against God's divine plan for humanity and nature, which results in conforming to an anti-God agenda and ignoring the injustice done by obediently following an oppressive ideology that will enslave civilization.

Let us not forget how Jesus stood up to the radicals and allowed the "truth" to be told amongst the deception during His era, despite the consequences; we, too, are not to ignore the injustice and deception surrounding us.

Washington D.C. & Jerusalem:

Presently, Washington D.C. resembles Jerusalem, as described in (Matthew 23).

The Power Elites of today can be likened to the Scribes and Pharisees living in Jerusalem during Jesus' era.

The Pharisees and Scribes are behind the arrest of Jesus during the Roman Empire.

Pharisees can be defined as those who are obsessed with power and exhibit hypocritical behavior.

They enforced strict and severe rules without making any effort to adhere to such regulations themselves.

(Matthew 23:4) tell us so.

If Jesus were here presently, how would He respond to the hypocrites in the nation's capital?

The Pharisees of our era – who are they, you might ask?

There are many political figures, and the legislative complex is overflowing with Pharisaical Hypocrites.

They enact unachievable, severe, and ruthless regulations.

Those who are unable to satisfy their standards are subject to harsh consequences.

Jesus' words in (Matthew 24:4) are being violated in the most extreme way imaginable.

"They crush people with unbearable loads and put them on other people's shoulders, but they are not willing to left a finger to move them."

Groups on the ideological left that seek things from individuals and companies and attempt to pressure them by threatening legal action or physical assaults are also portrayed as Pharisees, whom Jesus referred to for their corrupt behavior.

Other types of Pharisees in the modern era:

Members of the WEF, WHO, globalizers, radical judges, and CEOs from significant pharmaceutical sectors. Educated millionaires, operatives from the shadow government, and other heads of political factions.

The global warming hypocrites whose jets use energy in a single flight as a car used in a year are also part of the group.

They demand that society cut their electricity usage, yet they use vast power.

Liberal educators and college administrators, along with some medical officials, can be considered Pharisees in this era.

We are not exempt from Pharisees in modern times; it is fair to say they have increased.

When confronted with Pharisees at the nation's capital, how would Jesus respond?

He would address them as He did during the Roman Empire.

The modern-day Pharisees, however, have far surpassed their forefather in malice.

Comparing Jerusalem to Washington D.C. in the scriptures reading (Matthew 23), they are uniquely alike.

Jesus condemned Jerusalem for its' corruption of different factions within the city.

He would denounce Washington D.C. also, if not worse!

If Jesus were to walk the streets in the nation's capital

today publicly, He would proclaim to the Pharisees that he is God.

The Hypocrites would respond:

By what authority do you assert your claim to be God? That statement is highly resentful and politically incorrect. What you are saying goes against the decision made by the Supreme Court known as the "Establishment Clause" role in upholding secular Democracy's rule.

Jesus would tell them directly:

The Declaration of Independence does not reference the separation of church and state, so you are wrong; the "Congress shall not make any law respecting religion on banning the open practice thereof." By banning school prayer, the court overstepped its bounds and disregarded the charter's original intent.

If Jesus was confronted about abortion, He might answer:

Because of the Supreme Court's misuse of its authority and metaphorical reading of the Constitution, about 70 million innocent unborn babies have lost their lives in the abortion holocaust.

"Cursed to them that harm one of my little ones. It is better if a millstone is hung around their neck and thrown into the bottom of the sea than to harm one of my little ones."

The liberal mob responds:

It is a woman's right to choose.

Jesus would clarify to them:

Abortion is morally wrong and constitutes the act of taking a human life.

In the event of Jesus healing those who are afflicted and ill, how would the nation's authorities.

and those in the drug industries respond?

They would be outraged and suffer loss of income if Jesus healed people instead of resorting

to major pharmaceutical companies such as Pfizer, Moderna, J & J.

The companies would complain and criticize Jesus to the authorities.

The Pharisees were concerned about when Jesus healed individuals on the Sabbath day because it threatened their power.

(John 9:30-33) and other biblical passages tell us so.

If Jesus were to perform healing miracles today as He walked the streets in America, the pharmaceutical industry and government regulatory bodies would no doubt have a negative response.

2030 RESET AND DELUSION

On the UN website, they have outlined their plans and have on record a file for "transforming our world," which is to "Reset" the planet under their 2030 agenda that advocates facts on Individuals, the Earth, Wealth, Tranquility, and Organization.

Their Document Specify:

"In a spirit of mutual aid and cooperation, every nation and interested party will carry out this strategy. In addition to responding and protecting our world, we are determined to liberate humanity from the clutches of hunger and poverty. We will not stop until we move the Earth toward a resilient and environmentally sound future by taking the drastic measures that are sorely required. As we begin this shared endeavor, we ensure everyone will be included, and the goals and targets will inspire action in crucial areas for humanity and the Earth during the next 15 years."

The document was presented in 2015, and 2030 is the deadline for completion of their work.

It sounds like a great idea; however, if one has ever viewed the World Economic Forum (WEF) website, you will understand their real plan for humanity. I encourage you to visit their site.

It is the Utopia the Tower of Babel builders have always dreamed of. They believe they have reached god status and are the true guardians of the Earth, the world's gatekeepers.

When the wealthy globalizers of the earth own and control everything on the planet: Governments, corporations, institutions, transportation, food supplies, energy, military, banking systems, education, medical, entertainment, and everything else, they believe they own you as well; therefore, being the gods they think themselves to be, when their Tower of Babel (world government) is complete, you will serve them and no one, not one person is exempt. It does not matter what your political party is, race, occupation, or religion; all will be "serfs" to their system.

By what authority do I say this, you may ask?

The scriptures never lie. It does not matter if you disagree; it will still happen. It is written, and I believe God's Inspired Word over the Pharisees living in Washington, D.C., and elsewhere is accurate. They think they have reached perfection but will face a rude awakening.

God declares in His Word that a Fourth World Empire ruled by a wicked dictator over the entire Planet will be formed.

It is happening right before us; sadly, many are too busy, ignorant, or just flat-out not interested and could care less.

It is why we witness daily on news media, social media, and elsewhere the drastic measures globalists are taking to transform the old America most of us still love into a new America destined only for the Elite and those "serfs" that make it through, will serve the royal people living in their pretend Utopia of insanity and evil.

Influential tyrannical elites strategically influence the world's banking system through politico-geographical means, intending to establish an entirely new international system.

Once again, it is predicted long ago in the Book of Daniel, the Book of Revelation, and other prophetic books in ancient texts.

The 4th World Empire on Earth is presently being formed as the globalists "transform the world," they desire and are preparing for their beloved world leader to come on the scene. Still, before this happens, the world will be divided into ten regions with a leader (king) over each area. These will then hand all their power over to the coming world dictator, the Beast of Revelation 13, known also as the anti-Christ.

My previous book, "Narcissism Rising! The Final World Empire," discusses it in great detail.

As the prophets proclaim, conditions for the downfall of the Republic are steadily moving forward. At the same time, the scoffers and mockery are becoming more radical and hostile toward those of us who want to warn the masses.

It is why we have reached a point in society where the

radicals have flipped the "norm," calling the good evil and the evil good. That, too, was predicted in the scriptures.

Only those who have received a "reprobate mindset" can tolerate the evil we witness and call it good at this present time in history; they embrace madness.

They support and even flaunt their wickedness in the name of goodness.

Such individuals have turned their lives over to Lucifer, and it is why they feel no shame or remorse in their life.

The authoritarian global-minded and those that support them are the scoffers and mockers in this generation and go as far as cursing God on the holiest day of the year that Christians celebrate Resurrection Sunday (Easter), calling it "Transgender Day visibility."

Individuals taking such a strong stand, shaking their fits in God's face, follow the prince of the power of the air, also known as the father of lies, Satan.

A thick cloud of darkness has descended upon this country and world, just as in the Days of Noah; Jesus Himself warned it would happen, calling it "perilous times" in this last generation of end-time events, leading humanity into what is known as "The Great Tribulation."

(Isaiah 5:20) Is clear when it says, "Woe unto those who call evil good and good evil."

"Woe" means judgment in the ancient text and should be taken seriously.

Currently, in the year 2024, the ongoing conflict between good and evil persists.

It is a fight for the innermost being (soul) of both men

and women, and it will ultimately decide their eternal destination and their ability to choose freely.

The tearing down of the traditional America we all are familiar with and transforming our country and world into a "new order," a modern-day Tower of Babel, displays to us clearly in the Book of Daniel and Revelation a Fourth World Empire on Earth, thus, revealing to those who have biblical knowledge and understanding that we are indeed at the close of this present era on Earth as the Tower of Babel builders determine its completion by 2030, maybe sooner.

This "new order" is a game changer; that is, when all is complete, the average person will undoubtedly not be able to recognize the country they grew up in, as all traditional standards, values, and virtues will no longer exist.

Researching the ancient days of the early church shows us how many prophecies have already occurred, some written as far back as thousands of years before it happened.

There is no difference between now and then because what is written by men of old was inspired by the Holy Spirit; thus, what He says will indeed come to pass, despite what the doubters and rebellious try to dispute.

As the left in the country move at increasing speed to build their "new Tower of Babel" to reach heaven, just as the ancient group of people they follow thought they, too, reached god status, the result will be the same, but worse than their predecessors when God destroys the wicked.

The left is preparing the world we live in for the (Beast of Revelation 13), the antichrist, to take control over the

Utopia they want to establish. The Holy Prophets are always right, so you can count on it to happen.

It was recently reported that the left is using another tactic to dismantle the country: going after the Trucking industry by forcing truckers to transport their products in electric trucks, which no longer run on diesel fuel.

Biden announced he targeted gas stoves, other energy sources, and the trucking industry.

Dear friend, I pray you can see what is happening before us.

The assault on America is actual.

Taking such a bold step to go after the trucking industry will send this country back into a pre-industrial era.

Truckers are one of the most critical industries for a country's existence.

Without truckers, all essential products for your existence will be put on hold.

Talk is already circulating that it will force independent trucking businesses to close, and the larger trucking companies will not be able to survive.

The charging stations will be few and far between as it will make it impossible for the truckers to reach their destination; thus, you can count on empty food shelves, essential medicines such as heart, blood pressure, diabetes, antibiotics, and all other life-sustaining medications to be out of stock, baby formula not available, remember what happened during Covid-19 lockdowns, mothers were unable to get food for their children. Truckers could not move and just sat at the docks backed up, waiting to unload the cargo ships docked in the harbor for weeks because of the supply chain disruption.

COVID-19 was just a "test run" for what is in the making as we watch the eradication of this country.

Still, the "propaganda networks" will continue to broadcast to the public what a robust economy is and how the country thrives.

The lies will become more intense as the "spirit of the age" deceives the world into believing all is well, and the Beast of Revelation 13 will have no trouble winning the masses over as the rebellious will continue to harden their hearts.

(Revelation 13 & 14) all Earth dwellers will receive a mark on their right hand or forehead as they pledge allegiance to the world dictator. It will be mandatory to have the "mark" for one to buy or sell.

According to reports, digital currency and digital ID will become mandatory soon. It will be for the control of the masses and will be activated as a social credit system.

It is the technology used to gather information on everyone under the "new order," ensuring you are obedient to the "new system," as the banking systems are presently uniting, ensuring individuals can be tracked.

It is not the "Beast's Mark" yet, but the technology used, so when the "mark" becomes mandatory, the authorities can see who has it and who does not.

The left in the country and other leftist world leaders around the world have a dream they have wanted to make a reality, and now they are doing it, creating their new world system.

It is why there is a war on Christianity in this country and worldwide.

The elite wants to remove all traces of Christianity and the Bible. They understand their utopia cannot become a reality until the God of the Bible and all Christians are removed.

It is predicted in the scriptures that it will come to pass.

When the evil world dictator comes on the scene, the ancient text tells us he will hunt down all Christians and try to destroy the Jewish race.

Many who hold to their faith will be executed for not renouncing their belief in Jesus.

It will be a time of trouble like never before in the history of the world.

The Tribulation period is just before us, and the "signs" tell us it is coming soon.

God loves you and does not want anyone to perish, so He has made way for everyone to escape through His Son, Jesus.

If you are tired of your sin and searching for peace and happiness, you can receive salvation and forgiveness. You can be forgiven of all sin; it does not matter what you have done; Jesus will forgive you.

(Romans 10: 9-13) Explain it to you. Please read it and take the first step in receiving salvation. If you are sincere and take that first step, Jesus has already done the rest for you.

All Prophecy will be fulfilled concerning a one-world empire, the Reset of the planet, a new order, whatever one wants to call it.

The left in the country will continue to tear down the old and make their new order.

It is hard to know and understand what is unfolding before our eyes unless we know the Prophecy.

I encourage you to research it in the prophetic books of Daniel, Revelation, Isaiah, Jeremiah, and others. It is all there for anyone who has eyes to see and ears to hear.

{ **21** }

IS THERE ANYTHING LEFT

If someone wanted to bring America to its knees, could there be anything more disastrous than what is "fact" and what we have seen?

Let us sum up some past actions:

•Permit the unauthorized entry of 10 million immigrant nationals into the country, abolish all laws on migration at the national level, and allow the emergence of drug dealers and poisonous substances that kill over 150,000 citizens annually; label dissents using smear campaigns to injure and ruin their creditability.

•Belittle and insult those against the wasteful spending of continually adding 1 trillion dollars every hundred days.

•Seek forgiveness of leftist regimes for alleged previous American worldwide influence.

•Expedite the release of violent criminals with previous convictions without bail on the same day they are apprehended; pay attention to the murderer or rapist and feel sorry for them; completely disregard the victims and their families over the offender.

• Intentionally belittle some military personnel, label them as rebellion leaders and racists, discouraging them, with the aim of not serving and preventing them from reenlisting in the military, reducing the funding for military expenditures, and ceasing manufacturing of adequate weaponry, while leaving billions of dollars worth of arms in another country for America's enemies to apprehend.

•Employ strategies such as ballet destruction, proceedings of impeachment, legal lawsuits, and both national and state indictments instead of "Elections" as a means to overcome a political challenger, with the understanding that such people's lack of standards, policies, and integrity, don't have a platform to run on.

•Target the residences of Supreme Court justices who fail to comply with the demands of leftists.

•Switch to high-cost, undependable, and inefficient renewable sources of electricity, overlooking the fact that citizens will not be able to afford it and threatening to ruin the middle class financially.

•Presume respectable "alpha males" to be toxic.

•Raise your children to be ashamed of their race.

•Encourage young people who finish school and, upon graduation, dislike their culture and civilization intensely.

Such individuals are unhinged and without rational thinking.

The level of condescension displayed is astonishing, while the absence of law and order is clearly visible.

Who is really in control of the country?

Leftists are openly displaying fraudulent behavior without any attempt to conceal it, as it is a deliberate component of their "worldview" and who they follow.

When you contemplate the lawlessness and tremendous capacity to manipulate the legal framework so that it no longer serves as an institution of law, truth, and discipline and becomes an instrument for their governing dominance, their power becomes infinite.

As long as there is no resistance, the continuation of weaponizing the regime will persist into the greater dismantling of a country.

We have no one to blame but ourselves for being passive and allowing evil to triumph as Marxists/Communists control and have advanced in the war on the Constitution, Christians, Conservatives, Patriots, and anyone else on the right side of the political spectrum that upholds the rule of law.

As we continue to recognize the lawlessness, we remain in our comfort zone because it is just too hard to defend what is right, and if we lack courage and choose to allow corruption to play itself out, then we will enable the side of evil to advance in measures, that will ultimately destroy every freedom and the well-being of a nation, and a people.

Unfortunately, the cover-up of criminality and hypocrisy is bold and striking, and the intentional breaking of the system is complete, as the rule of law is no longer a reality but just a notion.

Have you ever thought that you would witness the dismantling of your country in your lifetime?

As assaults on the very fabric of our country and faith continue, is there anything left by the Left?

Of all the destructive steps taken by the leftist regime, the one that has most American Christians outraged is the bold and blasphemous declaration of Biden's "Transgender VisibilityDay."

It is not just Joe; most on the left are to blame.

Not long after Joe made the declaration, Nancy Pelosi and Kamala Harris also shook their fits in God's face by posting their support of "Transgender Day of Visibility" falling on Resurrection Sunday, March 31, 2024.

On "Good Friday," the day Christians observe Christ's sacrifice by a brutal death on the cross, Joe announced that all Christian themes on the Easter eggs would be banned for the following Saturday, which held the Easter egg art contest to be judged.

Be aware; It's not a coincidence that Joe and the party on the left chose the two most holy days of the year that American Christians observe, Good Friday and Easter Sunday, to proclaim "Transgender Day Visibility."

It was a deliberate and well-planned assault on American Christians and the belittling of Our Savior, the Lord Jesus Christ.

As they flaunt their evil around brazenly, the stench of

their depravity rises into the Lord's nostrils, and as (Isaiah 3:9) declares, it is a "witness" against them; God will repay!

Part of Joe's Proclamation"

"I, JOSEPH R. BIDEN JR.

President of the United States of America, by virtue of the authority vested in me by the Constitution and the law of the United States, do hereby proclaim March 31, 2024, as Transgender Day Visibility."

{ 22 }

A BATTLE TO SURVIVE

When Marxist rule, a symptom of an initial stage of illness, censorship, is the starting point of a developing problem.

It foreshadows the impending doom of assaults on the Constitution, the Country, and the People.

The acts prohibiting free speech serve as warning assaults, and acts of terror orchestrated by regimes are approaching.

Its initial stage begins with forbidding phrases or specific words; eventually, independent thinking is criticized. Marxist control allows "group think" only and forbids any other belief to be an enemy of the state. If you don't comply with their ideology, you face harsh consequences.

Next, rounding up individuals who are resisters to their "system" is a method used to imprison people.

When a system of law and order is compromised, panic and insecurity take precedence; the social structure becomes weakened by insurgency, and public support is overpowered by authoritarianism.

At present, a coordinated campaign to implement Marxism on a global scale is taking place in Western nations; it is referred to in (Revelation 13 & 14) as a world government run by the antichrist and his associate, the false prophet, and is to be complete by 2030.

It is why we witness daily transformations of our country as the regime continues to call for radical changes to "old America" as the puppet masters instruct their "New Tower of Babel" builders to move forward in the radical "Reset" and "Build Back Better" plan for the country.

An international "hierarchy goal" is to control the global governments and commerce by consolidating power and authority, and the intention is to terminate private ownership and complete dominance over all people with the aid of new technologies on surveillance.

Achieving their Communist agenda is what most Western countries are working toward, and surveillance on political resistance, occupying complete control of news outlets, penalizing disagreement, and overseeing and controlling discussions that take place in the public realm are all part of their plot to enslave humanity.

Liberal politicians are not concerned about 'weather changes". It is a handy tool used to progress their agenda; the primary objective is to gain mastery of every aspect of economic life by imposing an unfair advantage on resources.

The "signs" are clear; it is not about social justice, racism, a woman's right to choose, gender confusion, and everything else the left wants to put a label on; they are compelled to create "hate" and "chaos," thus, deepening the divide among societies, and falsifying the definition of civil liberties.

"Gun Violence" is not a concern by the mob on the left; they are resolute in confiscating all personal guns so that innocent citizens cannot defend themselves or their families against criminals and government tyranny.

Welfare dependency is what they prioritize for the public and getting rid of the middle class, so populations depend solely on big government.

"Wasteful Spending" is not a concern or integrity of the currency, inflation, and high taxes; it is a great tool used to break down the economy to implement a Marxist system to advance their control over all cultures and societies globally.

Alert! We are currently in the middle of a war for survival. If you have not recognized the changes already made and new ones announced almost daily in the country that don't benefit the public but increase hardships for families, perhaps it's time to do a reality check.

The "propaganda news outlets" remain silent on the drastic measures used to destroy the "old America" as the chipping away of every fabric of society continues to be affected by radicals advancing their evil utopia of world government.

Those concerned with getting "truthful" information resort to alternative news outlets; thus, censoring is present.

Marxists have argued over the years among themselves what is the best way to usher in their Communist Utopia:

Just wait for capitalism to dissolve itself or accelerate its planned Utopia by actively promoting social conditions to destabilize the Western world and its economy so that its "revolution" to fundamentally transform society will be complete.

A Communist Utopia is in the making.

Is there anything left in the country after the left?

I think not!

DO WE HAVE ANY RIGHTS LEFT?

Many wonder what can be done when tyrants are in control but let us first understand what one's "rights" really are.

Each of us has inalienable rights granted to us by God.

All of us have the right to defend ourselves from an aggressor.

When a confrontation with a home invasion poses a danger to yourself, your family, and your possessions, it is essential to safeguard oneself using whatever required means of response.

It works the same way when confronted by any aggression, including the nation-state.

Natural rights and laws are standards that are fundamental to humanity and based on natural fairness, but they cannot be violated, changed, or revised because of oppressive tactics.

No person has the authority to dictate to another person

what to eat, where to live, how to raise your children, and so on.

Everyone has the right to protect themselves from harm, no matter what type of harm, with whatever means possible upon force or encounter by the aggressor.

Individuals need to defend their lives, freedoms, and possessions.

It is essential to understand what it means when a government claims "they represent the people." You can consider past actions and whether they benefit or harm society.

•Do you feel safe in your community?

•Is your government doing everything possible to protect all citizens from domestic and foreign invaders?

•Are the citizens of this country that are homeless and disabled Vets being cared for?

•Do the citizens' needs of the country come first over others?

•Do you have Freedom of Speech, or are you censored in public expression?

•Is there a "Single" rule of law or "Two-tier" justice system in the country?

•Does your government uphold the Constitution?

•Do you consider "Elections" in the country legitimate without illegal interference?

•Is the economy prospering?

•Is inflation down?

•Have prices risen at the grocery store, utility bills, rent, gas prices, eating out, entertainment, etc.?

•Do you believe the public school system provides quality

education and that children are not gender confused about what is being taught?

•Do armed guards protect each public school in the country?

•Is there adequate funding for the military to be built up to defend the country?

•Are you in agreement with sacrificing the security of yourself, your family, and your country with an "open border" policy allowing terrorists to enter the country and, as a result, the head of the FBI putting out alerts warning American citizens they are at risk of a terror attack?

I could go on, but hopefully, you can make a realistic decision.

It is always best to pay attention to rules, laws, and standards that clarify your rights and not to be enslaved by a criminal organization seeking absolute control over society by coercion, physical tyranny, and forceful surrender.

A republic that respects its member's freedom is based on the notion that freedom is a God-given right, highlighting every individual's inherent dignity and freedom.

It does not create division using racial terms, which knowingly incites violence, chaos, or anarchy. It does not call for dismantling law enforcement, especially in high crime-rated cities and towns.

It always has the best interest of "all" its citizens, race, religion, and well-being.

Any political power that argues that society does not have inalienable rights granted to it by a higher power or natural law threatens the public by creating illegitimate statutes and rules used to dominate.

Freedom is not without cost, and it is vital to defend yourself, your family, your possessions, and your country against all acts of aggression, whether it be an individual trying to harm you or a criminal regime.

WORLD GOVERNMENT

As mentioned, a "One-World Empire" prophesied long ago is rapidly being constructed by the "New Tower of Babel" builders.

It will be a time when complete evil is released, and there will be no place to hide, as the prophets and Jesus Himself warned those with eyes to see and ears to hear.

We are the final generation to see the Lord Jesus' return, witnessing End-Time events rapidly developing and unfolding.

Under the New One-World Empire, it will be a time of trouble never before seen in the history of this country and world; so great a time of trouble, that as the Lord Himself said: If He did not shorten those days, no flesh would be saved (Matthew 24:22).

By gaining an in-depth knowledge of historical events that have come to pass and are still happening today, we can perceive what's to come with significantly improved insight.

It is almost impossible for anyone who has never

researched the ancient biblical history of prophetic events and those yet to come to pass to understand what is happening entirely before their eyes.

I encourage you to research the prophetic scriptures to clarify the subject matter and not be caught uninformed. The days are darkening and will grow much darker as the rebellious shake their fits in God's face and refuse His warnings.

As the ancient texts show us, God always forewarns a nation that judgment is coming, and He does not want anyone to be deceived or caught off guard. However, if a country "collectively" disregards His warnings, the unleashing of His Judgments occurs, and there is nothing anyone can do then because it will be too late.

Very few people in the country and world take to heart the warnings God has released and the many prophecies fulfilled but have been ignored.

Therefore, as (Romans 1) tells us, even though the truth is present, most people will ignore it. As a result, God gives them over to continue in their sinful behavior and allows them to be consumed by their wickedness, and they will receive a "reprobate mindset" by doing so.

A World Empire is being built as the "Old Empire" is "Reset" into a "New Empire." We see the proof of it daily as the news outlets, social media, and other networks show us, all happening rapidly, to be complete by 20230 or sooner.

Judgment is coming, and it will be unleashed in what is called the "Tribulation."

A World Government united by all cultures and

populations, enslaved by the "Beast of Revelation 13 & 14; this evil World dictator will proclaim himself to be god, and all the world will submit to his rule, taking his mark "666" on their right hand or forehead; all who refuse will be executed.

This and much more include massive earthquakes, pandemics, famine, 100-pound hailstones falling from the sky, asteroids hitting the earth, and the oceans, lakes, streams, and water supply becoming polluted.

God does not want anyone to suffer through such horror. It is why He made a way to escape through His Son Jesus.

(John 3:16) Explain what to do if you are sincere.

Jesus is coming soon, even closer than most realize. Don't be caught off guard.

A World Utopia is already halfway complete; don't be left behind when Jesus returns!

The world is full of darkness, but in the presence of darkness, light continually emerges victorious!

{ **25** }

SOLUTIONS & PREPAREDNESS

As conditions continue to deteriorate in our country, not knowing when the next pandemic, earthquake, or national emergency will occur, it would be wise to be prepared in advance.

Some suggestions can serve as a starting point to help maintain stability in a changing environment.

•Survival food: There are plenty of online sites that one can go to order "survival food." Another alternative is to stock up on canned foods, dry goods, and drinking water. Costco and Sam's Club are good places to find food in bulk.

•First aid kit: daily medicines, plenty of band aids, cotton swabs, hydrogen peroxide, rubbing alcohol, topical ointments,

•Baby formula: plenty of diapers, baby food, diaper ointment, toys for small children, coloring books, and crayons.

•Extra clothing and hiking shoes.

•Hygiene items: Soap, toothpaste, lotions, creams, feminine items, toilet paper, towels, face cloths.

•Sleeping bags: blankets, pillows.

•Paper plates: disposable silverware, garbage bags, and paper towels.

•Cleaning supplies: dish and laundry liquid, bleach, pale, sponges, etc.

•Flashlights: batteries, matches, propane, firewood, an axe, a camping knife, a tent, if you have one, a reliable barbeque, and water purification tablets.

•A weapon to defend yourself and your family and to hunt food if there are food shortages or no food at all. Plenty of ammunition.

•Most importantly, a bible that gives you all the answers to unanswered questions you may be searching for and peace in stressful situations.

In case of a national emergency, food shortages, etc., it would be best not to be in a densely populated area but a secluded area away from the cities or towns.

•Self-care: Prioritize mental, physical, and spiritual health during stressful times and understand that stress is a response we all experience during transitions and fear of the unknown.

•Financial Preparedness: Emergency Fund.

•Advocate Your Beliefs – Peacefully.

•Local Community Participation: Volunteering and supporting your city council, school boards, etc.

Routines: Try to continue with regular routines and incorporate new ones if possible.

•Hobbies and other activities incorporate into your daily activity to help you relax.

•Social Interaction: Impacts our self-concept and emotions.

•Connect with people you trust who have the same values and standards as you do. Let go of people who are not uplifting and harm you.

•Be mindful of how other's reactions affect you and set boundaries.

•Reevaluate your responsibilities and prioritize what's most important.

Relationships:

For your emotional well-being, staying in touch with family, friends, and neighbors with whom you are close and can share personal matters is essential.

Be open to forming new bonds with those you feel comfortable around.

AMERICA'S DECAY
& FALL

Abraham's nephew, Lot, lived in Sodom, and America appears to have reached the same level of debauchery, at least what I observe.

I am not happy to disclose this information. Even so, the unquestioned proof remains as it is, and to remain faithful to the purpose of sharing the Lord's truth that He declared, we can only do this by accurately documenting the events in our cherished nation that are happening daily.

Based on the story of the extent of wickedness in the twin cities of Sodom and Gomorrah, we can only speculate as to the levels of insanity that the inhabitants of Sodom had attained. However, Abraham and probably everyone else in the surrounding area became mindful of the dreadful reports concerning the two cities because it was so widespread.

Indeed, the iniquity was so great that it reached the celestial realm to such an extent that God descended to personally assess the magnitude of evil prevalent in the towns, just as He did when He observed the Tower Of Babel builders.

God, being infinitely aware, knows the beginning and the end of all things.

Still, it seems that He intended for Abraham and present-day believers to know that His understanding and thoughtful deliberation are not void when His judgment is implemented.

Many prophecy observers, including myself, continually wonder how much more a country can survive when it is so steeped in profound decay before God's catastrophic judgments fall.

Despite the apparent evidence of such vile degradation taking place in the nation, many still do not believe America has reached such a point.

Let us investigate, for instance, discussions on the social and cultural decay being legalized into U.S. legislation daily, which is quite concerning.

A Website, "The Washington Stand," featured a report: "Total Abomination: $1.2 Trillion Bill Funds Teen Trans Programs, Abortion to 22 Weeks."

The Bill features Queer 101 Training, Transgender Hormone Shots, Advertises Transgender Services for Minors, holds Drag Show Fundraisers, Transgender/LGBTQ+ Support, Hormone Therapy shots, LGBTQ puts illegals on a path to citizenship, Workshops on many Identities under the "Transgender Umbrella," Advertises "Drag Brunch," LGBTQ Senior Housing, Syringe Exchange, and more.

The complete and aggressive attacks on morality have undeniably resulted in tragic and harmful consequences.

The public education system, to a significant extent, exposes the children to the "Woke" ideology, which challenges God's established order, particularly in regards to the transgender movement and other morally objectionable behaviors that align with (Romas 1:28).

There is an awareness among those who diligently observe the "signs" as instructed that God's patience, built on His immense compassion, is approaching its full extent.

The current era, known as the "Times of the Gentiles," or "Church Age," is rapidly coming to its conclusion, and the era that features God's severe Vengeance and His Wrath is just before us.

We live in a society that is predominantly controlled by those who have effectively navigated down a path in which Satan has led them.

The path they are on leads them to a depraved mindset as a result of their rejection of God's mercy through His Salvation that they may have eternal life through His Son Jesus Christ, found in (Romans 1:18-27-).

When you receive a "depraved" mindset, you are no longer able to make reasonable, morally right choices, as well as rational decisions.

The Lord instructs us to "Watch," meaning those events that single His Return so that we are not caught off guard.

He explained this to His disciples when He sat upon the Mt. Olives when they asked Him what the "sign" of His return was.

The answer is found in (Matthew 24), but it refers to His second coming, not the Rapture of the church.

Simple point- No sign needs to be fulfilled before Jesus returns for His Church, as spoken of in (John 14). He explained to His disciples that He was returning to heaven to prepare a place for them, and He would return to receive them, and that where He was, they would also be there—those living in this era who have accepted His gift of Salvation.

He can return any moment in "The Blessed Hope," the Rapture.

If we already see many of the "signs" spoken of in (Matthew 24) such as earthquakes, pandemics, famines, and wars, about the second coming, how close can we be to Rapture?

As America continues a downward spiral, society becomes more depraved, "collectively speaking," especially when laws are enacted, such as what we are witnessing in this era.

God gives "signs" for us to "watch" and "warnings" to beware of if a nation crosses that invisible line He has drawn; two of such warnings are "Woe" to anyone who harms one of His little ones and those who dare divide his land and harm is chosen people the Jewish race.

I believe we are in trouble as a nation, as harmful rules and laws are imposed on youth and the land of Israel.

Jesus is Coming Soon. Be Ready!

NOTES

Chapter One: The Left of a Country

1 History & Society, Britannica, March 15, 2024. Madeline Davis, https://www.britannica.com/topic/New-Left

2 Hillary Clinton follower Sal Alinsky, Wikipedia, Hillary Rodham senior thesis, 1969, https://www.economicpolicyjournal.com/2013/04/hillary-clintons-1969-thesis-on-saul.html

3 Hillary Clinton "Mentor" Saul Alinsky Explored in Two New Films, Paul Bond, The Hollywood Reporter, Oct 27, 2016 https://www.hollywoodreporter.com/news/politics-news/hillary-clinton-mentor-saul-alinsky-explored-two-new-films-941304/

4 What is the connection between Obama and Sal Alinsky, Fox News, January 27, 2017 https://www.foxnews.com/transcript/what-is-the-connection-between-obama-and-saul-alinsky

Chapter Two: The Transformation of a Country

1 Obama unrestricted immigration, activists, What the Left Did To Our Country, Victor Davis Hanson, Sept 4, 2023, The Blade of Puscas, https://victorhanson.com/what-the-left-did-to-our-country/

Obama Anti Christian Bias, Critics: Obama's Words, Actions, Shows Anti-Christian Bias, Newsmax, April 9, 2015, Melanie Batley, https://www.newsmax.com/US/Barack-Obama-anti-Christian-rhetoric-easter-prayer/2015/04/09/id/637432/

Chapter Four: Open Borders

1 Terrorist Entering Country, How Our Open Borders Leaves Us More Vulnerable To Terrorism, AFPI, Kristen Ziccarelli, October 25, 2023 https://americafirstpolicy.com/issues/issue-brief-how-our-open-border-leaves-us-more-vulnerable-to-terrorism

2 Obama, End Of the Republic, Obama Goes All-Out in Final WHCD Speech: The End Of The Republic Never Looked Better, MEDIA-ITE, Josh Feldman, April 30, 2016, https://www.mediaite.com/tv/obama-goes-all-out-in-final-whcd-speech-the-end-of-the-republic-has-never-looked-better/

3 Biden border crisis, Comer Opens Hearing on Biden Administration Unilateral Actions Fueling Border Crisis, Committee on OVERSIGHT, January 17, 2024, https://oversight.house.gov/release/comer-opens-hearing-on-biden-administrations-unilateral-actions-fueling-border-crisis/

Chapter Five: A Cabal

1 Leftist Cabals Are Calling The Shots In America, AMAC, Jeff Szymanski, Feb 8, 2022, https://amac.us/newsline/society/leftist-cabals-are-calling-the-shots-in-america/

2 Covid Vaccine shots unsafe, Dr. Peter Mccullough, The Covid -19 Vaccines are not safe for Human Use, LINKED

in, The Wellness Company, https://www.linkedin.com/posts/twc-wellness-company_dr-peter-mccullough-md-mph-the-cvs-activity-7122570976990543872-coTW

3 Gateway Pundit, Archbishop Vigano Shares Powerful Message He Sent To Participants of "Medical Doctors for Covid Ethics International Meeting" Archbishop Carlo Maria Vigano, Jan 16, 2024, https://www.thegatewaypundit.com/2024/01/archbishop-carlo-maria-vigano-shares-powerful-message-participants/#comments

Chapter Seven- A War On Christianity

1 The White House, A Proclamation On Transgender Day of Visibility, March 29, 2024, https://www.whitehouse.gov/briefing-room/presidential-actions/2024/03/29/a-proclamation-on-transgender-day-of-visibility-2024/

2 PM. American News, Biden White House Bans Easter egg religious imagery from Easter egg art contest, Libby Emmons, March 30, 2024, https://thepostmillennial.com/biden-white-house-bans-religious-imagery-from-easter-egg-art-contest

3 Fox News, Pro-Life activist facing up to 11 years in prison; Peaceful Protest makes you a felon in Biden's DOJ, Kristine Parks, Feb 1, 2024, https://www.foxnews.com/media/pro-life-activist-facing-11-years-prison-peaceful-protest-makes-felon-bidens-doj

4 Newsweek, Acceptable Hate: Assaults on Christianity Go overlooked- Opinion, Shawn Carney, April 4, 2023, https://www.newsweek.com/acceptable-hate-assaults-christianity-go-overlooked-opinion-1791866

5 Critlarge, Hollywood's Disdain for Christianity, James Jeffery, Jan 18, 2020, https://www.critlarge.com/articles/2020/1/15/hollywoods-disdain-for-christianity

6 Catholic Exchange, Warning From Archbishop Vigano: Our Current Crisis & The Eternal Struggle, Archbishop Vigano, June 12, 2020, https://catholicexchange.com/warnings-from-archbishop-vigano-our-current-crisis-the-eternal-struggle/

7 Charisma News, Biden's Secretary Moves To Shut Down Largest US Christian University, James Lasher, April 18, 2024, https://www.charismanews.com/news/bidens-education-secretary-to-shut-down-largest-christian-university/

Chapter Eight, Prearranged Scheming

1"Contagion" Robert Ebert, Just Stand Over There and Wave, September 7, 2011, https://www.rogerebert.com/reviews/contagion-2011

2 "The City of New York vs. Homer Simpson," Wikipedia, Sept 21, 1997, https://en.wikipedia.org/wiki/The_City_of_New_York_vs._Homer_Simpson

3 Fatal Contact: Bird Flu in America (2006), Wikipedia, https://en.wikipedia.org/wiki/Fatal_Contact:_Bird_Flu_in_America

4 New York Post, Bird Flu pandemic could be 100 Times worse than COVID, Scientist warns, https://nypost.com/2024/04/04/us-news/bird-flu-pandemic-could-be-100-times-worse-than-covid

New York Post, Sen. Joni Ernst demands answers on Biden's USDA's $1M' dangerous bird flu

Experiments in China,

https://www.msn.com/en-us/news/politics/sen-joni-ernst-demands-answers-on-biden-usda-s-1m-dangerous-bird-flu-experiments-in-china/ar-BB1il3gP

6 New York post, Why ' Leave the World Behind' Viewers think the Obamas are sending a warning with the movie, Lauren Samer, Dec 18, 2023,

https://nypost.com/2023/12/18/entertainment/leave-the-world-behind-viewers-think-obamas-sending-warning/

7 ANP, Globalist Death Cult Tells Us What Next: No Internet, No Phone, No Power, No Food, No Going Back to Normal- Barack & Michelle Obama Produced New Movie Predicting TEOTWAWKI, Stefan Stanford, Dec 12, 2023 https://allnewspipeline.com/NO_Internet_NO_Phone_NO_Power_NO_Food_NO_Going_Back_To_Normal.php

8 Wikipedia, Apocalypse 11: Revelation, https://en.wikipedia.org/wiki/Apocalypse_II:_Revelation

Chapter Nine, Infrastructure

1 NEXTGOV, US power grid faces escalating cyber threats infrastructure experts warn, Chris Ricotta, July 19, 2023, https://www.nextgov.com/cybersecurity/2023/07/us-power-grid-faces-escalating-cyber-threats-infrastructure-experts-warn/388666/

2 US News, FBI said Chinese preparing to attack US Infrastructure, Reuters, April 18, 2024https://www.usnews.com/news/top-news/articles/2024-04-18/fbi-says-chinese-hackers-preparing-to-attack-us-infrastructure

3 Reuters, US warns hackers are carrying out attacks on the water system, Raphael Satter, March 20,

2024, https://www.reuters.com/technology/cybersecurity/us-warns-that-hackers-are-carrying-out-disruptive-attacks-water-systems-2024-03-20/

Chapter Eleven, The Playbook

1 MIT Technology Review, The Facebook whistleblower says its algorithms are dangerous. Here's why, Karen Hao, Oct 5, 2021, https://www.technologyreview.com/2021/10/05/1036519/facebook-whistleblower-frances-haugen-algorithms/

2 POLITICFACT, The word progressive... was created as a substitute for communist, Jon Voight, Oct 20, 2015, https://www.politifact.com/factchecks/2015/oct/22/jon-voight/actor-jon-voight-says-progressive-just-another-wor/

3 New York Post, How George Soros Co-opts the Media and Keeps Criticism Down, Matt Polumbo, Jan 26, 2023, https://nypost.com/2023/01/23/how-george-soros-co-opts-the-media-and-keeps-criticism-down/

Chapter Twelve, Marxism and Movements

1 THAIMBC, Klaus Schwab Rebrands Depopulation Plan as "Hum anocracy," Feb 15, 2024, https://www.thaimbc.com/2024/02/15/klaus-schwab-rebrands-depopulation-plan-as-humanocracy/

2 Britannica, Marxism, David T. McClellan, April 18, 2024, 3 New York Post, Black Lives Matter co-founder describes herself as a "trained Marxist," Yaron Steinbach, June 25, 2020, https://nypost.com/2020/06/25/blm-co-founder-describes-herself-as-trained-marxist/

3 Aero, Beware of the Trojan Horse: A

Critique of Social Justice, Gerfried Ambrose, June 19, 2019, https://areomagazine.com/2019/06/19/beware-of-the-trojan-horse-a-critique-of-social-justice/

4 Newsweek, Critical Race Theory is Repackaged Marxism Opinion, Liz Wheeler, June 14, 2021, https://www.newsweek.com/critical-race-theory-repackaged-marxism-opinion-1599557

5WEF, Klaus Schwab Releases "The Great Narrative" as a Sequel to "The Great Reset" Jan 2022, https://www.weforum.org/press/2022/01/klaus-schwab-releases-the-great-narrative-as-sequel-to-the-great-reset/

Chapter Thirteen, Climate Change

1The Free Library, The Frankfort School: Conspiracy to Corrupt, Farlex, March 1, 2009, https://www.thefreelibrary.com/The+Frankfurt+school%3a+conspiracy+to+corrupt.-a0195981116

2 The Conversation, Karl Marx and Climate Change, March 27, 2014, https://theconversation.com/karl-marx-and-climate-change-24896

3 VOX, There's less meat at this year's climate talk. But there plenty of bull, Kenny Torrella, Nov 30, 2023, https://www.vox.com/future-perfect/2023/11/30/23981529/cop28-meat-livestock-dairy-farming-plant-based-united-nations-dubai-uae

4 WEF, The UN says we need to reduce our meat consumption to fight climate change and improve food security, Stephanie Nebehay, Aug 9, 2019, https://www.weforum.org/agenda/2019/08/

global-meat-consumption-reduce-mitigate-effects-global-warming/#:~:text=Global%20meat%20consumption%20must%20fall%20to%20curb%20global,report%20on%20the%20effects%20of%20climate%20change%20concluded.

The Expose, Horizon Europe is a euphemism for technology, Rhonda Wilson, Feb 29, 2024, https://expose-news.com/2024/02/29/horizon-europe-is-a-euphemism-for-technocracy/

Chapter Fourteen, The Oligarch's Control

1 The Free Library, The Frankfort's School to Corrupt, Farlex, March 1, 2019, https://www.thefreelibrary.com/The+Frankfurt+school%3a+conspiracy+to+corrupt.-a0195981116

2 New American, The NOW Battle for North America, William Hakn, Jan 20, 2023, https://thenewamerican.com/opinion/the-nwo-battle-for-north-america/?mc_cid=bbb220d975&mc_eid=551904ee4c

3 Click2Houston, Explainer: Robert Arnold, Jan 6, 2022, https://www.click2houstoSo why is no one charged with a crime if Jan 6th is called insurrection? n.com/news/investigates/2022/01/07/jan-6-has-been-called-an-insurrection-so-why-has-no-one-been-charged-with-that-crime/

4 The Wine Press, Agenda 2030, You'll own nothing and be happy, Jacob Thompson, Aug 27, 2021, https://winepress-news.com/2021/08/27/agenda-2030-youll-own-nothing-and-be-happy/

Chapter 15, Lawlessness

1 Faith wire, Democrats Omit God From

Pledge Multiple Times At DNC, David Brody, Aug 20, 2020, https://www.faithwire.com/2020/08/20/democrats-omit-god-from-pledge-multiple-times-at-dnc/

Chapter 16, Depopulation & Media Control

1 Fox News, Founder of Soros-funded 'propaganda' news network, has visited Biden's White House over 22 times, Joe Schoffstall, https://www.msn.com/en-us/news/politics/founder-of-soros-funded-propaganda-news-network-has-visited-bidens-white-house-nearly-20-times/ar-BB1kVpsr

Chapter 17, The Breakdown of Society

1 All Sides, Biden Administration, ADMITS flying 320,000 migrants secretly into the U.S. to reduce the number of crossing at the border has national security 'Vulnerabilities,' March 6, 2024, https://www.allsides.com/news/2024-03-05-0334/immigration-biden-administration-admits-flying-320000-migrants-secretly-us

Chapter Eighteen, Despiteful of the Truth

1 The Daily HoldL, UN Proposes Digital ID System tied to Bank accounts and Mobil Payment platforms, Daily Hold Staff, June 24, 2023, https://dailyhodl.com/2023/06/24/united-nations-proposes-digital-id-system-tied-to-bank-accounts-and-mobile-payment-platforms/

2 Washington Examiner, West Point drops Honor, Country from its military statement, Asher Notheis, March 14, 2024, https://www.washingtonexaminer.com/news/2921117/west-point-drops-duty-honor-country-from-its-military-statement/

3 Heritage, The Rise of Wokeness in the Military, Tom

Spoehr, Sept 30, 2022, https://www.heritage.org/defense/commentary/the-rise-wokeness-the-military

4 npr, Laurel Wamsley, Transgender People to serve in the military, Pentagon releases new policies, March 31, 2021, https://www.npr.org/2021/03/31/983118029/pentagon-releases-new-policies-enabling-transgender-people-to-serve-in-the-milit

5 Lew Rockwell, If Any Out There Wants Freedom, You Will Have To Take It, Gary Barnett, April 10, 2024, https://www.lewrockwell.com/2024/04/gary-d-barnett/if-any-out-there-want-freedom-you-will-have-to-take-it/

Chapter Twenty, Diversity

1 21st Century Wire, The Globalist Billionaires and Their Plan to Wreck America, News Wire, March 1, 2023, https://21stcenturywire.com/2023/03/01/the-globalist-billionaires-and-their-plan-to-wreck-america/

2 Christian Today, The 2030 Agenda World Government, David, April 21, 2024, https://www.christiantoday.com.au/news/the-2030-agenda-one-world-government.html

3 United Nations, Transforming Our World: The 2030 Agenda for Sustainable Development, https://sdgs.un.org/2030agenda

4 The Hill, Biden Administration issues rule likely to push US heavy-duty trucks fleet toward EVs, https://www.msn.com/en-us/news/politics/biden-administration-issues-rule-making-more-new-heavy-duty-trucks-electric/ar-BB1kKC5V

5 New York Post, Biden has been shipping Migrants

to New York under Adam's Nose, Editorial Board, April 9, 2024, https://nypost.com/2024/04/09/opinion/president-biden-has-been-shipping-migrants-to-new-york-under-mayor-eric-adams-nose/

6 United Nations, "Replacement Migration," March 21, 2020, https://www.un.org/development/desa/pd/sites/www.un.org.development.desa.pd/files/unpd-egm_200010_un_2001_replacementmigration.pdf

7 belief net, 1963, Donna Calvin, Forty-Five Communist Goals in the Congressional Record, April 2011, https://www.beliefnet.com/columnists/watch-womanonthewall/2011/04/the-45-communist-goals-as-read-into-the-congressional-record-1963.html

Chapter Twenty-Two, 2030 Reset & Delusion

1 United Nations, Transforming Our World: The 2030 Agenda for Sustainable Development, UN, 2015, https://sdgs.un.org/publications/transforming-our-world-2030-agenda-sustainable-development-17981

2 The Hill, Biden administration issues rule likely to push US heavy-duty truck fleets toward EVS, Rachel Frazin, https://www.msn.com/en-us/news/politics/biden-administration-issues-rule-making-more-new-heavy-duty-trucks-electric/ar-BB1kKC5V

Chapter Twenty-Three, Is There Anything Left

1 Marxist, Marxism on the Rise in the USA, Oct 14, 2021, https://www.marxist.com/us-socialist-revolution-national-congress-2021-marxism-on-the-rise.htm#Perspectives%20For%20Revolutionary%20Social-ism%20in%20The%20Us

NOTES

Chapter 24, A Battle To Survive, The Heritage Foundation, How Cultural Marxism Threatens the United States and How Americans Can Fight It, Nov 14, Mike Gonsalez Katharine Gorka, https://www.heritage.org/progressivism/report/how-cultural-marxism-threatens-the-united-states-and-how-americans-can-fight

Chapter Twenty-Seven, America's Decay & Signs

1 The Washington Strand, Total Abomination $1.2 Trillion Bill Funds Teen Trans Programs, Abortion to 22 weeks, Ben Johnson, March 22, 2024, https://washingtonstand.com/news/total-abomination-12-trillion-bill-funds-teen-trans-programs-abortion-to-22-weeks

ABOUT THE AUTHOR

The author is a passionate student and observer of current trends of the day, both socially and economically, with a biblical perspective for over four decades. Her previous outreach programs were on social media and websites, and her most recent one is "Prophecy News and More.com," The author is the founder and organizer of a small church in Germany. At the same time, her husband served in the military. She enjoys outdoor time with her husband and fur baby, Nacho taking long walks at the beach, hiking in the mountains, gardening, cycling, and canvas painting.

The author is a researcher, writer, and news commentator on her popular website, bringing the latest news with accurate information you can trust.